BLIND SPOTS

BLIND SPOTS

A GUIDE TO ELIMINATING TODAY'S AUTOMOTIVE DIGITAL MEDIA WASTE

JEREMY ANSPACH

Published by Advantage, Charleston, South Carolina.
Member of Advantage Media Group.

ADVANTAGE is a registered trademark, and the Advantage colophon is a trademark of Advantage Media Group, Inc.

Printed in the United States of America.

10 9 8 7 6 5 4 3 2 1

ISBN: 978-1-64225-226-2
LCCN: 2021909085

Cover design by Megan Elger.
Layout design by Mary Hamilton.

This publication is designed to provide accurate and authoritative information in regard to the subject matter covered. It is sold with the understanding that the publisher is not engaged in rendering legal, accounting, or other professional services. If legal advice or other expert assistance is required, the services of a competent professional person should be sought.

Advantage Media Group is proud to be a part of the Tree Neutral® program. Tree Neutral offsets the number of trees consumed in the production and printing of this book by taking proactive steps such as planting trees in direct proportion to the number of trees used to print books. To learn more about Tree Neutral, please visit **www.treeneutral.com**.

Advantage Media Group is a publisher of business, self-improvement, and professional development books and online learning. We help entrepreneurs, business leaders, and professionals share their Stories, Passion, and Knowledge to help others Learn & Grow. Do you have a manuscript or book idea that you would like us to consider for publishing? Please visit **advantagefamily.com**.

To Ford, for giving my grandmother a job as an immigrant on the assembly line. She was always proud to work for "Fords."

To my dad, for having a passion for muscle cars, especially those from the '60s, when cubic inches and fire-breathing big blocks reigned supreme. His dream muscle car was in the garage during my entire childhood—and it has now taken four generations for a ride.

To my mom, for driving me to every car dealer in metro Detroit after I got my learner's permit as a teenager—because I was determined to test drive every car made in order to document the showroom experience.

To my wife, for believing in me and trusting I could help the auto industry thrive—and for supporting me as I founded, supported, and grew PureCars to an industry leading company.

To our COO Jeff Ranalli, our Senior Director of National Accounts Lauren Donalson, and our Director of Product Marketing & Sales Enablement Matt Copley for their help in guiding this book to completion, as well as the entire team at PureCars for making great stuff happen and always doing whatever it takes to help the auto industry thrive through innovation and transformation.

And finally, to the dealers who have attained such a high level of entrepreneurship that they have literally driven our industry's success to unparalleled heights. Yes, there is always room for improvement, but I will never waver from saluting your accomplishments.

CONTENTS

FOREWORD

BY RHETT RICART, CEO, RICART AUTOMOTIVE

2020 NADA CHAIRMAN

After I had the good fortune to read an advance copy of this book, I immediately called up Jeremy Anspach and said, "This is a book that every dealer principal should be required to read."

As CEO of Ricart Automotive, I know that how we market is critical to our success, as I'm sure it is to yours. The problem is, it's hard to know whom to trust, especially when it comes to digital. Most of the people who run dealerships are no spring chickens (yours truly included), and this is a whole new world to them.

A lot of companies out there take advantage of this lack of knowledge by trying to sell dealers systems they just don't need. Here's a statistic that might blow your mind: in recent years, *70 percent of the vendors at the annual NADA Show have been software providers.* That's huge. And that percentage is so high simply because these companies know that dealers are frantically looking for digital solutions that work.

Unfortunately, most dealers don't know enough about digital to know what data they need or how best to put it to work. The result? Most dealers are left to try to sort out a fire hose of information that leads only to more confusion. They're being sold small pieces of the digital marketing puzzle that do little, if anything, for them all by themselves.

My nephew Rick Ricart, our director of retail operations, brought Jeremy Anspach in to talk with us, and the moment I heard how he talked about what he did for his clients, I could see he was someone who really loved dealerships and genuinely *wanted* to see them succeed. He and his PureCars team weren't about smoke and mirrors; they were about *results*, and how digital could help us achieve them. If an idea of his didn't work, he was the first one to throw it aside and look for one that did—which was refreshing after experiencing other vendors who would cash the check, send us their software, and disappear into the night, not being all that concerned about whether their products really boosted our revenues.

What he's done with this book is remarkable. He's simplified the concepts for the average person in a powerful way, so you don't have to be an expert in digital to get what he's talking about. And that's a great gift for every dealer. This book is what you need to finally get ahead of the curve and keep ahead on this technology that's constantly changing—because it contains evergreen ideas that go beyond grabbing at the newest bright and shiny piece of tech. Instead it focuses on big picture solutions to how we need to be selling cars in this day and age.

I want to emphasize that Jeremy's perspective is incredibly important simply because he is a car person. All he and his team want to do is help dealers up their store's game. That's something I got from my first meeting with him, and I haven't seen anything to change my mind after years of working with him, because our numbers just keep getting better and better.

As I said at the beginning of this foreword, this book should be required reading at every dealership. It should be read by every general manager, marketing person, director of digital operations, and on and on down the line. The landscape has changed forever, and we have to change with it.

Let this book serve as your guidebook to navigating that change.

INTRODUCTION

O ne of my earliest memories of school was sitting in "Circle Time." The teacher asked all of us what we wanted to be when we grew up. And everybody before me gave the answers you'd pretty much expect at such a young age.

"Doctor!"

"Fireman!"

"Astronaut!"

Then it was my turn. And I'll never forget the look in my teacher's eyes when I said ...

"Car dealer!"

Weird? Yeah, a little. But to be fair, I grew up in the shadow of the Motor City, Detroit, Michigan, surrounded by car iconography, like the giant Uniroyal Tire my family used to drive past on I-94. It seemed bigger than anything else in the world—and cars seemed like the biggest deal in the world, in my estimation.

I think my passion was initially triggered by one of my father's most prized possessions, a 1967 big-block Corvette. Because it was already sitting in our garage before I was born, I grew up watching my dad uncover it, prime the carbs, and crank the ignition time and time again. When that engine roared to life, it hit me where I lived. I was hooked. That muscle car was awesome, but—and I know this is going to sound *really* weird—the sound, the smell, and the experience of my dad's car really made me fall in love with all things automotive. Thinking about it, I can trace that feeling back to my grandmother, an immigrant who had worked at Ford. She held enormous pride in her job on the assembly line putting together windshield-wiper motors, and that pride never left her to the day she died. That pride deeply touched me.

So, to me as a boy, cars were more than just cars. They were an obsession. And for those who thought I'd grow out of it … well, they turned out to be very wrong.

As a teen, I lived for the moment when I would become fourteen years and nine months old. Why was that exact age important? Because in Michigan at the time, that was when I could get my learner's permit. But that was just the gateway to my *real* plan. I wanted to go out and test drive just about *every single vehicle* sold at the metro area's dealerships.

My pitch to my mom was that it would be educational for me. Yes, I still wanted to be a car dealer, and this way, I could see how they all did business. And of course, I could drive some cool cars without paying a penny for the privilege. Thankfully, my mother humored me, and by the time I turned sixteen and could get my real full-fledged driver's license, I had learned a ton about cars and how dealers worked. It was obvious to me even then that those who demonstrated transparency really made a difference, a better impact, and today those dealers continue to lead.

So now you're probably waiting for the payoff. "Tell us about your dealership, Jeremy. How did you do with it?"

Well, here's the twist—I never bought a dealership of my own. However, I did help dealers sell more cars, but in a completely different way than I ever imagined. It was still the early days of the e-commerce era when I discovered that my natural talents bent more toward the digital advertising side. I saw a whole new world of cyber-based marketing opportunities opening up, and that excited me as much as the world of car dealerships.

So it just made sense to match up my passions and shoot for the stars.

THE INFORMATION REVOLUTION

I realized, along with a whole lot of other people, that the internet was mostly about information—more specifically, the ability to have it at your fingertips. For example, with cars, you no longer had to go to the library and read back issues of *Motor Trend* or get your own copy of *Kelley Blue Book* to find out about car specifics. All that data and more was starting to appear on websites.

And I couldn't stop thinking about how I could leverage that kind of information in the dealer's favor.

My first effort in this direction was a start-up named Servit, which provided dealers with a tool that enabled customers bringing their cars in for service to see what their vehicle needed in terms of maintenance. Prior to Servit, service advisors sometimes misled customers on what they needed, due to sloppy paperwork or neglecting to access the previous history of work on a customer's vehicle, which led to problems. Work that had been recently done was duplicated, simply because the car had gone over, say, thirty thousand miles. Or work was not done that should have been, resulting in vehicle issues and even breakdowns. Trust gets lost with that kind of haphazard approach.

I created Servit in the early 2000s to eliminate those glitches by blending the factory- and dealer-recommended maintenance items into a reliable digital tool, so customers could be assured that the service their vehicle was getting was the service it actually needed. This didn't hurt dealers; it actually helped them—because at times what the vehicle needed was more than the customer expected. At the same time, they couldn't deny *that* they needed it, once they saw it all on a screen in color with great detail about both the dealer- and factory-recommended maintenance schedules.

Result? The dealer was able to raise the average customer pay repair order substantially, which naturally generated more revenue from what was already a big profit center, the service department. But even though the dealership might be making more from customers as a result of our program, they were actually building *more* trust with them, because they were tracking their service history and requirements in a new and more professional manner. That kept the vehicle running more efficiently, which made customers feel more confident in their purchases, which increased their satisfaction scores. And it was a perfect example of what I wanted to do—provide critical on-site information that was missing from the picture and could improve the dealer's profitability. After all, if people could *see* what maintenance they needed to have done at that point of their vehicle's life, they would feel obligated to follow through on having the work done.

You would think this should have been a slam-dunk product that dealers would immediately eat up. A no-brainer. And yet, this was the first time I really ran into how powerful dealership blind spots were. They had been selling and servicing cars a certain way throughout the twentieth century, they had been making a lot of money, and they weren't really interested in changing things up, even though the internet revolution had already begun.

I found this out for myself when I began to try to sell dealers on tapping into digital marketing, as well as our Servit service tool. I had been running my own small e-commerce business near the end of my high school years and all through college, selling niche-market motorcycle parts and accessories. I wanted to use the expertise I gained from that experience to help dealers thrive by bringing them into the digital age.

But they weren't all that into it … at first.

I remember my first attempt like it was yesterday. I had actually convinced a large Chevrolet dealer to trust me with helping them build an internet department. However, when I began to try and recruit salespeople on the lot to participate, they treated me like I was radioactive. No one wanted to get involved, except for one computer geek who loved tech and was the only one pulling leads from online sources.

Well, what a difference a few months made. The internet department caught on and grew to the point where, when I would come visit this dealership, the salespeople were suddenly jumping in front of me at the front door, asking if they could be a part of it. They were suffering, because the other sales guys who were using the internet were getting more foot traffic than the ones who weren't.

I personally witnessed how digital could drive more profits for dealers. So after Servit was acquired by a private equity group in 2007, I looked around for other areas where information would make that kind of difference—but on a much bigger canvas. My research uncovered the fact that dealers invested over $700 per used vehicle on reconditioning (putting on new tires, brake pads, etc.) in order to make them "stand tall." They spent that money because it was a great selling point for customers who came to the dealership—the salesperson could point to all the improvements and impress the customer.

The problem was, with the internet, that selling point was suddenly lost. More and more consumers were checking out cars online, where there was no indication any of these improvements had been done and, therefore, no motivation for customers to choose one dealership over another.

Again, information could turn around that situation.

I founded PureCars in 2007 with that goal in mind. We created what millions of consumers know as the PureCars Value Report, which showcases the key value, options, and reconditioning attributes of a vehicle. Those reports were then posted on our subscribing dealers' websites next to a picture of the vehicle, so the consumer could *see* what had been done to improve it. Now the dealers' cars could "stand tall" online and that $700-per-car investment in reconditioning fees would actually drive traffic to the dealership. And it worked. The dealers enjoyed more conversions. On our side, it represented the first step in building an extensive digital database identifying consumer shopping patterns. That large proprietary data warehouse we built gave us the opportunity to jump in with both feet to create digital dealer advertising that fully exploited the internet's potential.

So in 2013, we launched SmartAdvertising, which quickly became the leading digital advertising technology for dealers. Today, it's one of the largest in the industry, and it continues to expand because it provides a huge benefit to the industry. Thanks to our database (which to this day, continues to grow), dealers could see for themselves which vehicles they should be aggressively marketing, which target markets were best for them, and which media channels would be most effective in reaching those markets.

Result? Dealers could make their ad budgets go a lot further by paying a lower marketing cost per vehicle sold.

For most, great tech is nice—but somewhat like a toolbox, it still needs a skilled and knowledgeable craftsman to use it effectively. At PureCars, we worked hard to become those kinds of high-level craftsmen in applying tech to dealer objectives, and as a result, success came fast for us. PureCars won the 2013 Driving Sales Innovation cup and was acquired by Raycom Media in 2015, making the list of the top twenty transactions in the year, according to *Forbes*.[1]

> Great tech is nice—but somewhat like a toolbox, it still needs a skilled and knowledgeable craftsman to use it effectively.

We caught on due to a simple fact—nobody was using data at the level of sophistication we were in automotive. At the time, other marketing vendors were selling "automated marketing" to dealerships. All that really meant was they identified keywords for each vehicle at the dealership and worked those keywords online. But a lot of nuance was lost in that too-simple system.

The truth is that some vehicles are priced more effectively than others. Others are merchandised better. And some are in such high demand and low supply that they'll sell quickly without additional marketing dollars. Any system that didn't take those kinds of factors into account ended up wasting a lot of money—and many dealers still don't, owing to the "blind spots" we will explore in this book.

In this book, we will help you learn how to overcome those blind spots and prosper in the process. But before you flip the page and go to the first chapter, I just want to emphasize that I know your

---

1   Alex Konrad, "How One Advertising Startup Far From Silicon Valley And NYC Scored A $125 Million Cash Exit," *Forbes*, November 4, 2015, https://www.forbes.com/sites/alexkonrad/2015/11/04/how-purecars-sold-for-125-million/?sh=3672e6ec2ad1.

business, I love your business, and I want it to thrive. I have built some of my best friendships in the dealership business, and I respect what incredible entrepreneurs you all are. I also respect how important you are to your community, in terms of providing jobs and spearheading local philanthropic efforts. So let me be clear—this book isn't about reinventing the wheel; it's about improving it. I'm confident you'll find many of this book's key concepts valuable enough to implement and that when you do, you'll be more than happy with the results. Our clients, who run the gamut from Jaguar, Porsche, and Mercedes-Benz to General Motors, Honda, and Volkswagen, as well as numerous independent dealers, certainly have been.

One last note: If you're a dealer, you may be thinking I'm writing this book to sell you on PureCars. That's not my intention. Instead, I want to share *ideas* we have learned through working with the thousands of dealerships who have used PureCars and provide strategies to help you take your marketing to the next level, so it becomes both more effective and less costly. In short, we want to unlock opportunities for you that you may not be aware even exist—opportunities that will boost your margins, increase revenues, and grow more success for your dealership.

My dream is to keep the dealership model alive, so consumers don't all end up having manufacturers deliver cars to them directly.

Here's my bottom line. I'm as excited about cars as I was when I was a kid. And I'm excited to show you how you can sell more of them with fewer marketing dollars. My dream is to keep the dealership model alive, so consumers don't all end up having manufacturers deliver cars to them directly. I also know the importance of dealers to their communities. To keep that dream alive, we all have to keep moving forward, rather than be left behind by ever-evolving technology. I hope you'll use this book as a guidebook to systems that have been proven to increase sales and profits. And I wish you all the success in the world on that journey.

Best,

Jeremy Anspach

CHAPTER ONE

BLIND SPOTS

WHAT YOU COULD BE MISSING

*Don't look back and ask, "Why?" Look
ahead and ask, "Why not?"*
—NEIL PATEL

A dealership in the northeast US was the largest dealer of its brand in its state, as well as in the top ten of the entire nation. But a few years ago, they were on the decline and knew they had to change things up. So they made a change. They came to our company looking for some high-powered digital solutions that would truly optimize performance in real time. Wasted marketing spending suddenly became a thing of the past, as we worked with their team to maximize ad efficiency wherever possible based on customer demand and market insights.

The results spoke for themselves.

Suddenly, the dealership had no shortage of traffic or leads. They began selling more cars than they had ever sold and, at the same time, saved $30,000 in marketing costs. They were now running a coordinated multichannel media strategy and making daily decisions based on the data collected from each customer interaction. Their digital advertising impact was maximized, and at the same time, spending become much more cost-efficient. Through utilization of a data-driven mindset, the dealership was able to accurately pinpoint areas of opportunity to pull in prospects from other dealers and grow revenue.

During their first quarter working with us, we helped our client dramatically increase VDP Views (257 percent), leads (209 percent) and sales (17 percent) from digital campaigns. In addition to helping them exceed sales goals for new and used inventory, we also launched Waze ads for them, which drove 57 percent more service and repair leads. A few other stats are highlighted in the graphic below:

CTR
▲
+22%

CPC
▼
-20%

CONVERSIONS
▲
+71%

CALLS
▲
+33%

MONTHLY SPEND
▼
-20%

VEHICLE SALES
▲
+17%

358
DIRECT NAVIGATIONS
to the service bay
from Waze Ad

The above true case study illustrates the power of digital when it's properly deployed, even when you're already a dominant number one store. The dealership had a feeling that's familiar to all of us by now—they couldn't keep marketing the way they had in the past. It wasn't working anymore. They came to us for a reboot, and we were happy to help.

Now, here's the good news. The concepts behind that remarkable turnaround are the concepts you're going to learn in this book. And when they're correctly implemented, you can experience some amazing results, like the results reached in the case study above. They even achieved their big goal of becoming a national force in their brand's sales.

As I noted in the introduction, this book is about identifying blind spots in dealer marketing strategies and giving you the tools to overcome them, so you can spend less on marketing and at the same time drive more sales.

You may think that's a pipe dream, but it's more than possible—the power of digital marketing has been proven many times over. It provides bulletproof methods that allow you to realize the maximum value of each of your vehicles. We're going to talk about those methods in this book.

But first, let's look at where most dealerships are at this moment in time and why digital marketing is so critical to their ongoing success.

THE STATE OF THE DEALERSHIP TODAY

When it comes to dealerships, there are a couple of other things that are obvious, at least to me.

First, it's obvious to me you know your business. Otherwise, you wouldn't still be in business. Dealerships are run in a way that differs

13

from most conventional businesses, so they require a unique expertise that's born of experience. I learned that quickly when I was a teenager, and it's part of why I love them. They're still an outlier in an age of mass branding and commoditization. And I can certainly understand it more than, say, the mattress business.

Second, it's obvious—probably to both of us—that the retail car business has become much more challenging. As much as the internet has been a boon to most industries, it's dealt a big blow to car dealers. Thanks to the explosion of online information over the years, consumers now have access to almost as many details about cars as the dealers themselves. What's more, those consumers can bring that information up on their smartphones right at the point of purchase and challenge a dealership employee on everything, including price, quality, incentives, service intervals, recommended maintenance … the list goes on.

And that's why, for over a decade, dealer margins have been eroding on both new and used vehicles. What used to be the classic dance between customer and salesperson has morphed into a flat-footed fact face-off. When they know as much about your vehicles as you do, you no longer have the advantage when it comes to making a deal. Some people think *car dealer* is an outmoded term because there's so much less wiggle room in negotiations that the actual "dealing" has been minimized. In other words, throwing in rustproofing isn't going to do the trick anymore.

What's also obvious is how many disruptive entrepreneurs are trying to reinvent the entire car-buying experience through app-based technology that allows and even encourages consumers to avoid car dealers altogether. While I don't believe dealerships are going to go the way of the dodo, these are still new avenues of competition that can't be ignored.

The upshot of all this is you no longer have a license to print money. Every dollar you spend has to be accounted for. And that dollar has to be targeted to bring in more dollars, or you're throwing money into the wind.

Which brings us to marketing.

Before the internet, dealer marketing dollars were locked into conventional media—billboards, TV commercials, radio, and newspapers, not to mention the occasional giant inflatable ape placed on top of the dealership roof. Advertising was based on such familiar tropes as a car dealer yelling, "Come on down!" while wearing a stars-and-stripes jacket or a superhero costume in a TV commercial. Nobody was more of a master of this approach than the legendary Cal Worthington, known throughout Southern California for appearing in ads with his so-called dog Spot. I say "so-called," because in those commercials Spot was never a dog but one of a variety of exotic animals—a tiger, a seal, an elephant, or even a hippo. And back then, you couldn't argue with that approach. In 1988, Cal, with the help of Spot, grossed $316.8 million, making his the most successful dealership chain of all time at that moment.[2]

But that was 1988, and this is thirty-plus years later. Yes, this kind of marketing is still done today to raise name recognition, but it doesn't significantly raise profits. Even though people may know and like a dealership as a result of successful branding, that does not in any way guarantee it's going to be their first stop when they go to buy a car. Today, most consumers are savvy enough to research the best price before they even set foot on a car lot. It's just too easy to do the legwork by sitting in your bed and doing searches on your smartphone.

---

2   Stanley, Don. "The Dealer: By Golly, Cal Worthington Went from Dirt-Poor Ranch Hand to Millionaire Car Czar," *The Sacramento Bee*, January 14, 1990.

So—how do you combat the fact that potential customers are able to easily target the best deal before they even start shopping? Simple. By targeting *them* when they're on their smartphones.

Your only chance to flip the script is to use the data as strategically as they do so you can lower your customer acquisition costs as well as the cost of marketing each individual car. That's an essential step toward long-term profitability, because margins are probably going to continue to tighten. Instead of broadcasting, you want to think about narrowcasting—by placing the right ad for the right car in front of the right customer at the right time. Amazon's been doing this for years, and there's no reason dealers can't replicate the success of these techniques. Our team helps them do precisely that.

DEALER BLIND SPOTS

Yes, it's true that most dealerships put the bulk of their marketing dollars into digital these days. But many of them aren't leveraging the data to the extent they could. Frankly, they often don't have time to think about it.

Even the best managers are easily overwhelmed by the day-to-day operations of a dealership. The auto-sales industry is highly competitive and too often, tunnel vision kicks in. Your focus on what you sold that day, week, or month, rather than taking a global look at how your marketing can have more impact. And even though you may think you're doing everything possible to merchandise your cars digitally, that world keeps evolving in such a fast and furious manner that you lose track of innovations that literally change the marketing landscape.

This is what leads to blind spots referred to in the title of this chapter. During our work with clients, we routinely identify their blind spots, and after they're addressed, they see the benefit. That's how we know these blind spots are real and that they stand in the way of maximizing revenues. Shining a light on them is a guaranteed way to improve an already-thriving operation and take it to new heights. And it's also a way to turn a struggling retail dealer into a winner.

I'll be honest. Sometimes it drives us absolutely crazy to see a dealer missing what we believe to be impactful marketing methodologies. But then we have to remind ourselves, this is *our* core business, not the core business of a dealership (which is obviously to sell and service cars). With the proliferation of digital media channels popping up left and right and all the technology and tools that are now available, we have to work our butts off to keep up with all the newest methodologies ourselves. Since you have much more on your plate, it's understandable that these blind spots can develop.

However, they *do* develop, and they're the real deal. We've had the privilege to work with thousands of dealerships for over a decade and have identified five of the most common blind spots we run across.

BLIND SPOT #1: "MUSCLE MEMORY"

I cited Amazon as a prime (no pun intended) example of a company that has leveraged digital marketing to the max. They've built an e-commerce site like no other, and the foundation of their success is how they market to their customers. You've probably had the experience of searching for a product on their site, then finding to your surprise an ad for that exact same kind of product while scrolling through your Facebook feed or another social media platform. That's Amazon putting the data to work.

Amazon was able to revolutionize this kind of marketing because the company is relatively new and came of age along with e-commerce. It made sense for them to not only be open to it but take the ball and run with it. After all, they weren't tied to a past when there *was* no internet marketing. They started from scratch and rightfully focused their efforts on what advertising would bring them the most targeted traffic.

Car dealerships, however, *do* have a long past—the first one opened its doors in 1898 (in Detroit, of course ... and by the way, it sold only electric cars). And there are traditions to dealership marketing, some of which I've already cited—outrageous, attention-getting radio and TV commercials, as well as billboards, direct mail, and newspapers. That's the advertising most of today's dealers grew up with, and that's where the "muscle memory" cited in this blind spot enters the picture.

Muscle memory is usually a good thing. We learn a skill or pattern by repetition until it becomes second nature. We no longer have to *think* about how we do something; we just do it. The classic example is someone with the same rigid daily commute who, one night, has a different destination to drive to after work, such as a restaurant where they might be meeting friends for dinner. But on the way, that person starts to daydream, and before they know it, they're pulling into their driveway at home instead of the parking lot of that restaurant, because they guided themselves on unconscious instinct.

That's the power of repetition and the power of muscle memory. While muscle memory is invaluable in most tasks you do repeatedly, it can sometimes work against you, like it did with the commuter we just referred to. There are dealers who reflexively downplay sophisticated digital marketing because it's still relatively new and complex. Traditional media is what they understand, so traditional media is what they emphasize. But traditional media can't be instantly changed or recalibrated. ROI measurement is also difficult to impossible, because you can't get the kind of detailed and clear real-time data that you can retrieve through digital marketing.

Obviously, dealers can't completely ignore online marketing. They know they've got to have a website with all the bells and whistles, that's a necessity these days. However, they still might think the giant billboard they've had up on the freeway for decades does the best job. You can push back by saying Amazon uses traditional media, too, but the fact is Amazon doesn't rely on it for the bulk of their marketing. Their operation doesn't have that muscle memory, and they don't have a past to cling to.

> It's human nature to stick with what works the best. The danger is when you stick with what *used* to work the best.

It's human nature to stick with what works the best. The danger is when you stick with what *used* to work the best and don't open yourself up to new ways of doing things. Luckily, despite the adage, "You can't teach an old dog new tricks," we've worked with plenty of dealers who have embraced the new technology and upped their game as a result.

It's great to watch it happen.

BLIND SPOT #2: PUTTING BUDGETS BEFORE RESULTS

Businesses run on budgets. I get that. And most businesses, including dealerships, have traditionally set finite budgets for various marketing initiatives. I get that too. What I don't get is why you would stop investing in a money-making ad run before you've made as much as you could from it. This again is a case where repeating what you've done in the past can actually work *against* your business goals.

From what I've seen, the car business still runs on an ad budget that is a fixed number, set annually, quarterly, or in most cases, monthly. When that budgeted amount is determined, then a marketing manager or general manager decides which vendor will get what percentage of the budget.

This fixed-budget mentality is ingrained in our system because of the way we were taught to buy traditional media. However, with digital marketing, there's a big difference because you can track your ROI to the penny. Having those metrics at your disposal means you can make some very informed—and very profitable—decisions on the fly. And that means when a particular digital ad run is working and still bringing in money, you don't want to put an arbitrary limit on what you spend on that campaign. That's like shooting yourself in the foot. Why not keep investing in that marketing if it means it's going to make you more money?

This again is another one of Amazon's secrets. They do not market on a fixed budget. They keep spending until thresholds are met for each product—and that threshold is when demand outstrips supply, because at that point, you have nothing left to sell until it gets restocked. In other words, they don't leave money on the table. And I'm sure you don't want to either.

So trust the data. And as long as you're getting a return, keep spending. Don't go into the month thinking, "I'm going to spend $20,000 in digital advertising this month, and that's it." If you end up spending $45,000, but the money you brought in more than makes up for the extra expense, why worry?

A finite budget causes two pain points. In some cases, it erodes profitability due to overspending on media that doesn't pay off. In other cases, it damages profitability due to *under*spending on marketing that has a strong ROI—because you pulled the plug too soon.

The guiding principle for a dealer should be, "I can spend up to *X* number of dollars to acquire a customer for this vehicle in order to produce a good margin. If I'm continuing to acquire those customers through my marketing, then I should keep spending that X number of dollars until my supply chain breaks and I no longer have that vehicle to sell."

In other words, why turn off the spigot? Why not keep the money flowing in order to make *more* money?

BLIND SPOT #3: VENDOR CHURN

Some dealers change marketing vendors abruptly because they expect it will change their results. They look for a miracle, someone who will come in and tell them how they'll sell more cars than the other vendor they're currently using. They dangle shiny objects, and the dealer quickly latches on to them if they're having a bad month.

It's very, very common. It's how our company wins business, and it's also why we lose business (fortunately, the latter happens way less frequently than the former).

When you switch vendors too often, you're constantly rebooting your marketing and not giving your current efforts a chance to pay off. A solid vendor needs time to prove their worth, because they have to use tech to see where there's room for improvement and what messaging works best. Because of that steep learning curve, your dealership loses whatever momentum it had in terms of sales when you switch vendors. So there's a real cost to that kind of vendor churn, especially if the new company can't deliver.

The best alternative to this is to thoroughly check out a vendor before you sign on the dotted line (or, more common these days, the virtual dotted line). Read reviews and talk to other dealers who use the vendor. Most importantly, set a baseline of attributes you want the vendor to bring to the table in order to meet your marketing goals. And make sure they have a data-driven approach. Don't buy into someone simply claiming, "I'm going to sell more cars for you for less money." Make them *show* you how they're going to do it.

But before you do that, think about why you want to switch vendors. What's missing that you're looking for? Dig in and figure it out, so you're not just switching for the sake of switching, because it will be a big operational headache you probably would rather avoid. You don't want to end up like Sisyphus from Greek legend, the poor guy who pushed a giant boulder up a hill every day, only to have it roll right back down to the bottom. That went on for an eternity—and none of us have that kind of time!

BLIND SPOT #4: A WHOLE NEW WORLD

Yes, that's the title of a famous Disney song. But it also perfectly describes what sophisticated digital marketing feels like to many dealers. It's a whole new world, and that can be a scary proposition, especially when the discipline has grown to such complex heights. You can't expect to understand all its ins and outs unless you work directly in the field.

To put it mildly, digital advertising is harder to grasp than traditional media. It's much more immediate and offers an overwhelming array of options. There are literally thousands of different combinations of search ads, display ads, and video ads a vendor can employ on your behalf. And you can't possibly review them all, because, clearly, that vendor is not going to sit down with you in your office and show you, say, the ten thousand different online ads they're running. That meeting might continue overnight and into the next day.

Checking out a couple of TV spots is, of course, a completely different story. You can review them in a few minutes and be done. Also, you grew up watching commercials; it's not as if they're a foreign species. Effective digital marketing, on the other hand, can feel like something very alien. Those who hire companies like ours often don't even know the right questions to ensure their new partner is deploying the best strategy.

This isn't a putdown. Again, this is expertise that's hard won. Many clients try to frame it in the same way they frame conventional media. They bite down hard on a few familiar and broad-based KPIs (Key Performance Indicators), and that becomes the way they measure success with vendors like us. As a result, they ask, "How many impressions did you make? How many leads did you create? What's the cost per lead?"

All good questions. But sometimes they should be asking, "Did you market the right vehicles on my lot? Did you target them to an area that gives me the maximum likelihood for not only the sale but also the servicing of that vehicle once they buy it? And were you able to lower my cost per vehicle sold?" These are real goals digital can reach. Amazon thinks that way every day, as do a whole lot of other merchandisers.

Some clients get stuck on how to lower marketing costs. They'll ask, "Can you get the price per click down on our Google ads?" Well, hell, yes, that's easy, you just need to bid on lower-priced keywords. But again, you might just be incurring a new self-inflicted wound. A high-priced term means it's more popular and more people are searching for it. So if those keywords directly relate to a model you need to sell, you absolutely should be bidding on them, as long as you don't go over what your ad cost per unit sold is for that model.

Digital differs from traditional media because it's all about *high frequency*. And because it's high frequency, it's harder to feel it and it's harder to see it. There might be a different ad for every type of vehicle on your lot, and each ad will have different parameters depending on which model it's designed to sell. Those ten thousand ads can also provide an overload of data that can explode your brain if you don't know what to focus on.

So it's much easier for dealers to focus on rebates, cash coupons, newspaper ads, and the kind of marketing you can touch, feel, and "get" with a glance. But digital advertising also reaches a whole new world of consumers who are targeted because they're perfect prospects to buy the car you want to move off the lot. We'll get more into the weeds of how we market vehicles right down to the VIN number later on in this book.

BLIND SPOT #5: IGNORING LIFETIME VALUE

As I've said, I've interacted with thousands of dealers. And I never heard one of them mention the lifetime value of a customer. Most of them, again, are focused on how many cars they sold last month—and how many of those vehicles they can attribute to our marketing on their behalf.

The lifetime value is the overall net profit you can expect from a customer who ends up staying loyal to your dealership car after car, for whatever reason. Maybe they like the brand of vehicle you sell. Maybe they live three blocks away and like the idea of walking home after leaving the vehicle for servicing. Maybe they have a personal relationship with a manager or salesperson. Whatever the motivation, recruiting as many consumers as possible with the most potential to offer you repeat business is obviously crucial to a dealership's long-term prosperity. Recurring revenue from those consumers bringing in their cars for service every few months is a critical underpinning for any successful dealership. Just as Apple is now emphasizing service-fee bundles to keep customers paying month after month, you, too, want to avoid focusing on one-time buyers you may never see again. Getting that repeat business should be a top concern.

With digital targeting, you can make that happen. And maybe that's why many dealers don't think about it, because traditional marketing can't do it as well. But most business leaders *do* think about lifetime value and make it a pivotal part of their efforts. Customer acquisition costs go down as you accumulate more and more customers with a high lifetime value. And for a dealership, that means focusing on buyers who are likely to bring their cars right back to your service department for maintenance and eventually trade in the original vehicle you sold them for a newer model. Or get a car for their spouse. Or a car for their kid. To quote another Disney song, you end up with quite a "Circle of Life" that way.

But that circle may not complete if you don't treat your customers right.

According to *Auto Trader*, 54 percent of consumers want to buy from a dealership that offers a preferable experience, even if it didn't offer the lowest prices. In other words, a majority considers how they're treated to be more important than cost. So … don't go for a short-term win at the expense of gaining a long-term customer. Let's say you manage to overcharge a customer, say five thousand on a vehicle that you normally make only a thousand on. You may feel like patting yourself on the back, but when that customer realizes they're upside down on the equity they have in the car far more than they should be, you won't see them again. It's penny wise, pound foolish.

Here's a fact you are probably already aware of. A decade ago, a customer visited an average of 4.5 dealerships before making a buying decision. Now? It's down to 1.3. In other words, many customers who show up at a car retailer have come ready to buy. The sale was pretty much made before they ever walked through your doors.

What does that tell us? That the real battleground to win car buyers' hearts and minds is now in cyberspace. And your best weapon on that battleground is digital marketing. From my experience, that's obvious. Dealerships need to employ it and make a transformational shift in looking at data through measurements they can trust and understand. Making the right digital marketing company part of your team will help you do that.

> The real battleground to win car buyers' hearts and minds is now in cyberspace.

These blind spots are ones we help our clients address every day. And in the remainder of this book, we'll help you address them too. In the next chapter, I'll discuss the transformational "brain shift" dealers need to make in how they actually execute their advertising—through unique and powerful methods which will be revealed in the remainder of this book.

REFLECTION EXERCISES

(Note: At the end of each chapter, I'll be asking a series of questions to help you take a hard and honest look at how your dealership scores in terms of the content I've just shared. This isn't meant to be a test; it's meant to spur thinking in new directions to improve your marketing results).

1. How would you compare your marketing to competing dealerships in the area? Do you feel you're falling behind or are ahead of their advertising efforts?

2. How sophisticated are your digital marketing efforts? Do you or does someone else on-site have enough of an understanding of digital marketing to use it effectively?

3. Is your vendor giving you the support and information you need to make the right judgments? If not, can you request they deliver data in a way that's easier to digest?

CHAPTER TWO

IT'S ALL IN THE DETAILS

ADVERTISING DONE RIGHT

The aim of marketing is to know and understand the customer so well the product or service fits him and sells itself.
—PETER DRUCKER

Dealers, of course, aren't the only one with blind spots. Drivers have them too. Which is why the car companies have made big investments in technology to compensate for them. New vehicles have all kinds of "smart" sensors designed to prevent accidents that used to occur when the driver was unable to physically see another vehicle, object, or even a person. This technology enables the vehicle to "see" it for them and either warn the driver or simply stop the car at once in order to avoid a collision.

As noted in the last chapter, marketing blind spots develop because dealerships are preoccupied with their day-to-day business, which, as you well know, can be very demanding. But just as today's technology can help a driver cope with blind spots, it can also guide a dealer to the best possible marketing results. It's a different type of tech to be sure, but just as reliable if used correctly. Digital data can help dealers "see" things that they otherwise would have missed, such as misappropriated advertising dollars, opportunities to generate more revenue, and prospects who could provide the most long-term value to their dealerships. That's the basis of our foundational strategy to help you sell more cars, realize higher revenues, and develop more loyal customers. And at this time in our history, it's more important than ever for dealers to go all in with this technology, rather than see it as a necessary evil.

In this chapter, I'm going to introduce some broad concepts that our company lives by in helping dealerships spend less and earn more from each car sale. As you continue through the book, you'll find more specifics that will allow you to implement these ideas in a practical on-the-ground manner through the use of digital tech.

Dealership marketing has dramatically shifted to digital since internet marketing first took hold. That transformation has accelerated thanks to the COVID-19 pandemic. Because car buyers weren't able to visit showrooms when everyone was on lockdown, digital marketing became more critical than ever before, and a lot of dealers who had been reluctant to fully embrace digital had little choice but to give it a big ol' hug. After all, according to the latest Google data, 83 percent of car purchasers spent up to three months doing research and are ready to buy when they arrive at your door![3] So when I tell you

---

3   Thomais Zaremba, "The auto dealer's guide to navigating today's digital landscape," Think with Google, February 2021, https://www.thinkwithgoogle.com/future-of-marketing/digital-transformation/auto-dealer-guide/.

online is where you need to be, those numbers scream to the heavens that I'm not exaggerating—especially when many start-ups are out to entirely eliminate dealerships in the car-buying equation.

Obviously, this is a critical time for dealers. And yet, according to *Forbes* magazine, the auto industry is lagging behind other industries in terms of online marketing, even at a time when they need to do more of it than ever before.[4] Why? Because of the Muscle Memory "Blind Spot" I identified in chapter 1. Dealerships (and the car manufacturers themselves) tend to invest too many marketing dollars into TV ads, even though a lot of that audience has shifted to ad-free streaming services (another trend that has only increased since the pandemic began). Even those who do sit through TV commercials are usually multitasking when they pop up between program segments. They're checking their phones, getting a snack or a drink from the kitchen, or doing what many people have traditionally used commercials for—a bathroom break.

Here's the bottom line on advertising (and another set of numbers that might rock your world): research shows that traditional advertising such as radio spots, TV ads, and billboards bring in an average total profit of $1,702 per vehicle, while digital marketing brings in $2,514 per sale. That's adding over a third more total dollars to your margins. The same study also found that it costs $150 of digital marketing to sell one car, compared to $1,581 in traditional media.[5] In other words, you could end up paying ten times more than you have to if you rely heavily on outdated marketing. Meanwhile, most of your

---

4   Tom Treanor, "Why Automotive Marketing Is Changing and How to Meet the Demand," *Forbes*, September 10, 2020, https://www.forbes.com/sites/forbescommunicationscouncil/2020/09/10/why-automotive-marketing-is-changing-and-how-to-meet-the-demand/#663cdb49a3dd.

5   "5 data-driven strategies to acquire more customers," BHPH Report, February 16, 2016, https://www.autoremarketing.com/bhph/5-data-driven-strategies-acquire-more-customers.

customers are looking for cars online, not offline, and COVID-19 has only increased that trend. Here's another statistic to back that up: *10 percent of new vehicles sold in 2020 were sold online, compared to just 1 percent in 2018.*[6]

I'm not saying traditional media is going to completely disappear. It will remain in the mix for most dealers, and it should. But overall, when a potential customer is on the web looking for their dream car, your emphasis *has* to be on finding a way to put your vehicle, instead of the competition's, in front of their eyes. You want them to see that dream car listing at *your* dealership. And if you do end up in the search listings next to theirs, which is probable, you want to make sure your vehicle "stands tall" when compared to theirs.

In the last chapter, I called out the blind spots that I feel many dealers suffer from. In this chapter, I want to show you what we at PureCars consider "Advertising Done Right." Hopefully, you'll gain an understanding of how we, in the words of a famous Steve Jobs Apple ad campaign, "Think Different" about dealership marketing—and discover the huge advantages adopting this viewpoint can deliver to your business.

MARKET SHARE

Before we get into Advertising Done Right, let's talk a little about the importance of market share.

Dealers gain momentum just by becoming the market-share leader in their particular area. They become known as a dominant (and hopefully trusted) "brand," a dealership everyone in town knows

---

6   The Top Dealer Guidebook 2.5, https://docs.google.com/presentation/
     d/1s6GmCoDZLdrHd1AM94c_cdjqWQMjPkVioCG7BsUKcgw/
     edit?resourcekey=0-7aLBquhi5ii6wOpdWHsA9g#slide=id.gbbfa55631a_0_981.

and respects. If you've ever watched the series *Friday Night Lights*, think about how the character of car dealer Buddy Garrity casts a large shadow over the town where the high school is. Buddy may be written a little cartoonish, but a lot of the details about his business are right—his dealership is shown to be a powerful component of the local economy and community because of its branding, sponsorships, and employment opportunities. When you're in the Buddy Garrity position, your dealership is more poised to make a sale than the competition.

It all comes down to name recognition. When you're buying laundry detergent, for example, and there's a container of Tide versus some brand you never heard of, and the price is the same or close to it, you're probably going to choose Tide and not the kind you never heard of. This is why dealers with high market share often "win the click" online. The consumer recognizes the name, knows that dealership has a strong reputation and wants to see what they have to offer, before taking a deep dive into less well-known lots.

What we normally find in that scenario is that guy who's the market leader really has it figured out. He may make very little per unit because he is selling at a lower cost, but he makes it up in volume, volume, volume. That enormous volume then gives him a huge vacuum to pull those buyers into his service department again and again. That's a big blessing, because service is generally a big profit center for a dealership. And if it's run well, service sets up customers to go right back to sales to buy their next vehicle. It ends up being a very powerful circle.

Dealerships want to capture market share. We've never been in a meeting where the dealer says they're not interested in that. Most want to create that name recognition that automatically generates a positive association, because it weaponizes their marketing and gives them an edge the other dealers can't match. And that's an important advantage to have in a time when sales margins are decreasing and competition is increasing.

When you engage in Advertising Done Right, you have every chance of increasing your market share, because you will wind up boosting sales and customer traffic. That, in turn, will lift overall awareness of your brand.

Think about Amazon (and I'll be asking you to think a lot about that company in this book). A lot of people don't even think much about price when they buy from Amazon. They assume they're getting a deal, especially if they're a Prime member and enjoy that two-day free shipping (which more and more has become one-day shipping with no extra cost). Amazon is so dominant it's just the go-to for millions who need something in a hurry and don't want to hit the mall or search endlessly at other e-commerce sites.

But Amazon didn't get to that point by accident. They did it through the kinds of systems I'm advocating for in this book. Those systems empowered them to build the biggest and best online store in the world. Why shouldn't you want to benefit from those kinds of strategies?

With that in mind, let's get into what we consider to be Advertising Done Right. It all starts with asking three questions.

THE THREE QUESTIONS YOU MUST ASK YOURSELF

In the past, advertisers looked for places where they could simply get the most eyeballs on their ads. If that meant a giant billboard on the freeway or a commercial in a popular high school football game, then the advertiser would pay what it took to get that kind of powerful placement.

Now, however, it's no longer about where you can get the biggest audience. Most of those people driving by that billboard, for example, aren't in the market for a car (maybe because they're already in one!). *That's why it should be about targeting the attention of those who are actually in the market for a car.* Think about an election poll. Which is more useful—finding out what percentage of all registered voters are going to support a candidate? Or what percentage of *likely* voters are going to support them? It's pretty clear which is preferable. It does no good for a campaign to know what someone who isn't going to the ballot box thinks. Their focus has to be on who *is* going to vote—and what will motivate them to go for their candidate. In politics, that's an obvious marketing strategy. And it should be for dealers too. Why waste money spending big to reach a huge unfiltered audience, when most of them aren't interested in buying a car and won't be any time so soon? Especially when it's a whole lot more cost effective to target consumers who (a) ARE ready to buy and (b) have the potential to have a high lifetime value.

There are three big questions that inform Advertising Done Right. They are:

1. What are you marketing?

2. Who do you want to target with your marketing?

3. Where is the best place to reach those potential customers?

These three simple questions lead you to answers that help you do advertising right.

Let's start with question one: **What are you marketing?** What are the odds of a Ford dealer running a full-page ad saying, "The 2021 Bronco, come on down and check it out." Well, all the odds are against it, because that vehicle hasn't been released yet (as I'm writing this, anyway). It would be irrational to pay big bucks for that ad. And you also don't see dealers promoting the fact they have twenty used cars for sale without listing prices or posting pictures of the vehicles. Why? Because those vehicles aren't ready for showtime yet.

These are easy open-and-shut scenarios that dealers wouldn't engage in. But some dealers do make similar mistakes when it comes to marketing specific vehicles. That's where logic must come into play. More questions have to be asked, such as,

Is my day's supply high enough to justify spending to market these vehicles?

Do I know my cost-per-vehicle-sold break-even point for each model I'm spending ad dollars on?

Do I really need more people to look at this car? Or is the demand for it so high, it's likely to sell without me investing any resources into marketing it?

Are the cars I want to market priced well? Or am I going to be stuck with these overpriced units ninety days from now?

What's the best marketing channel for merchandising this car?

By considering your stock more closely before you market it, you can make more intelligent marketing decisions. All vehicles are not created equal, and marketing them all the same means you could be losing some possibly powerful leverage.

Here's how we addressed an inventory challenge for one of our clients, a Toyota dealership located in the northeastern US. This store had a specific and unique inventory challenge in late 2018. The store depleted their core model inventory and, at the same time, received an influx of new Corollas. The store typically averaged six Corolla sales each month. Now, however, based on their inventory and sales objectives, they needed to sell twelve Corollas in one month.

They first looked at their engagement-score metrics through our Signal tool (Signal is a data-driven, multitouch attribution solution that uses a unique model to weigh the value of digital channels—paid and unpaid—for Return on Advertising Spent, or ROAS, and sales) and determined that the Corolla, their most highly stocked new car, had a low engagement score, even though the model had plenty of online views.

When reviewing engagement-score metrics provided in the Shoppers section of Signal, we noted that the dealership's most highly stocked new car, the Corolla, had a low engagement-score. While there was plenty of online interest and Corolla received many search results page (SRP) views, shoppers were not viewing vehicle detail pages (VDPs) or submitting lead forms. After further investigation, we found that our client's advertised lease price was the highest in the area.

After the dealership updated their price to better align with the market, we analyzed market reports based on YTD Corolla purchases and advised our client on the areas to target for sales. Our team then cultivated and deployed a Corolla-centric marketing campaign. All of these strategic adjustments paid off for them. the dealership sold eighteen Corollas that month, 150 percent above the monthly sales objective.

That's just one example of how you can target a specific model and improve your results.

Now, let's move on to the second question: **Who do you want to market this car to?** If you have a used Lexus that's often sold to, say, a fifty-five-and-up group, that's a very different target than some twenty-two-year-old looking for a Jeep Wrangler two-door sport vehicle. You have to play your own version of *The Dating Game* to match up the right car with the most likely buyer.

With that in mind, let's take that basic "who" query to its logical conclusion through a series of focused questions, such as,

Who is the audience for this car?

What's the best way to appeal to them? Price, prestige, or our location?

What will motivate them to act?

When you understand the target market for each type of vehicle, that puts you a step ahead in devising the right marketing strategy.

The third question, **Where is the best place to market to reach those potential customers?** should inspire the same question-and-answer process to help you decide what marketing channel will get you the best results. Ask yourself things like this:

How do I reach locals with a high potential lifetime value?

What digital channel (Facebook, Google Search, Instagram, YouTube, etc.) offers the lowest ad cost per unit?

How frequently do I confirm that is still the case to be sure I don't have muscle memory bias to media channel performance?

How do I get the most direct traffic for those looking for this car?

Where is the demographic I'm targeting most likely to be when they are close to making a purchase decision?

Basically, it comes down to taking your best shot at reaching the demographic in your area that has the highest probability of buying what you're selling. But that's only half of it. You want to also make available to that person a direct link to that vehicle page on your website. Remember, if you do focus on a specific vehicle, you have much better odds of getting a click than, say, a store selling washing machines. Dealers have the advantage of selling specific models people are familiar with and actively looking for. Washing machines, not so much.

Advertising Done Right happens when an established dealer dominates the direct online traffic from sources that give that dealer the opportunity to drive that traffic directly to their dealership website. That dealer has to be willing to spend more on search terms that will generate more sales, because that's how that domination happens. The dealer also must always be maximizing the merchandising component. If you win a click, you can also win a conversion if the consumer ends up looking at a car listing with a high level of transparency, quality photography, a good description, and a good deal. Those factors enable you to be 100 percent optimized for conversion and increase the probability of a phone call, an email, and ultimately an in-person visit. Again, we'll go more into detail on this type of sales funnel in a future chapter.

> That dealer has to be willing to spend more on search terms that will generate more sales, because that's how that domination happens.

ADDRESSING THE BLIND SPOTS

In the last chapter, I identified five big blind spots that I see many dealers suffer from. When you're doing advertising right, all five end up being addressed.

- Dealers will no longer rely on "Muscle Memory" (#1) once they've created a robust digital strategy.

- They'll see how going over budget on a certain campaign will actually more than make up for the extra expense with increased revenue, so they will stop "Putting Budgets Before Results" (#2).

- "Vendor Churn" (#3) won't happen as frequently if dealers understand how to use data well enough to choose a marketing agency wisely …

- … which means they will have become comfortable with the "Whole New World" (#4) of data-driven marketing.

- And finally, any sensible dealership digital strategy has to target customers with a potential high lifetime value—so "Ignoring Lifetime Value" (#5) will no longer be an ongoing concern.

But to avoid all five blind spots, Advertising Done Right has to be a concept that's integrated into every part of a dealership and put into practice on every single business day. Follow-up is all-important. I can't tell you how many times I've worked with dealers who spend considerable time and effort to acquire the kind of traffic we just talked about in the last section, through TV, radio, billboard, direct mail, and digital. And then they hear consumers say things like, "I called three dealers who had the car I wanted, and they never answered the phone." Or "They said they would call me back and never did." Integration is also important. All departments of a dealership—service, sales, marketing, and financing should communicate between each other the hard information needed to get the marketing job done.

Now more than ever, dealerships have to be responsive at every level. And they have to put as much information online as possible. What we've learned from this pandemic is consumers want it easy. They want to do as much research online as possible until they're ready to come visit your physical space. That research can take a long time because vehicles are now so complicated. They all have different technology available, different power trains, and different features and options. And most consumers want to know about all of it, so they can make an informed decision. That's why I think the best dealers are the ones who have successfully removed the wall between their physical and virtual spaces—with an exceedingly high level of transparency. They also make the transaction as easy as possible for the customer. In other words, they return phone calls. *They are responsive.*

Dealers also should consider expanding their understanding of what data means, both in terms of providing it to prospects and analyzing marketing results. In the first instance, we need to understand what information should be emphasized in order to move the needle for the average consumer. In the second instance, we should pinpoint what advertising is most effective, both in terms of branding and in terms of selling specific cars.

Here's the equation that counts more than any other right now:

Data-oriented = Profit-oriented

Dealers who have either someone on-site with the expertise to accurately analyze or a vendor they can trust to read the numbers for them have a leg up on the competition. I'm sure you're aware that attracting and converting customers is a puzzle that has to be solved every day, sometimes with different solutions than the day before. Reliable and executable data is central to making the best decisions and achieving the best results consistently over time.

> Reliable and executable data is central to making the best decisions and achieving the best results consistently over time.

***

This is just an overview of what I believe represents Advertising Done Right. In the next chapter, we'll go from the theoretical to the practical and dig more into the details of using data effectively at your dealership. This isn't something Buddy Garrity had to deal with back in the day—but something today's dealers must not just accept, but buy into fully and make a priority.

REFLECTION EXERCISES

1. How does your market share compare to other dealerships in your area? How are you working to increase it?

2. How well are you answering our three questions with your marketing campaigns? Do you understand the details as we described them as the "What, Who and Where?" of your advertising?

3. Do you have someone available with extensive data expertise to help you crunch the numbers and judge your results realistically? Is that person on-site or a vendor?

CHAPTER THREE

DATA VERSUS INFORMATION

I'm not worried about good numbers or bad numbers. I worry about the process.
—MAX SCHERZER

"**W**hat do the numbers say?"

How many times have you heard that question? As a businessperson, probably around a million times. But here's the thing: the numbers don't really say a damn thing. They're just numbers. And only someone who understands what's behind those numbers is qualified to speak to what they mean.

Numbers are data. An accurate assessment of what they signify constitutes information. And in our business, there is no more important distinction than the difference between the two.

In this chapter, we're going to break down the difference between data and information and apply these principles to dealership marketing. From the subject matter we're about to discuss, you'll gain a better understanding of what type of knowledge is going to help you increase profits—and what type is just going to leave you shaking your head in confusion.

DATA IS NEVER ENOUGH

As you may have gleaned from the beginning of this chapter, data is generally all about raw numbers. Information is an interpretation of those numbers , an interpretation that takes into account context and outside influences—and if that interpretation is correct, it will guide you in making the right moves with your marketing, sales, or whatever is on the table.

> Data is generally all about raw numbers.

Because we do so much digital advertising at PureCars, it's easy for us to generate a tsunami of numbers with a few keystrokes. Way too easy. And if we aren't selective about what numbers we examine, we could waste day after day sifting through mountains of data that would leave us and our dealers overwhelmed and clueless. Yes, it's nice to be able to download all sorts of permutations of data with all kinds of variables. But when anything is possible, sometimes nothing gets done, simply because you end up lost in an infinity of choices.

And this, in fact, is what happens with many dealerships. They can get bombarded with data and can't see the forest for the trees. When they're getting ninety reports from ninety different vendors, obvious things become not so obvious. The vendors don't talk to each other, and it's up to you to try and figure out what it all means. That task is made much more difficult by discrepancies in all that data. It's not always proven. It's not always understandable. It's not always reliable. And it's rarely executable.

Think of it this way. Let's say you turned off that fire hose of data and you walked into your dealership blind. And then you started rebooting only the systems that you need to succeed. What systems would those be? And how would you want to consume the content? This is a mindset we try to adopt on a daily basis. We want to be in a position where we give dealers the data in a way where it's useful information that's executable, stacked in the most relevant way, and given to them in the easiest way to digest. Is it an email? Is it a text? Is the frequency changing based on how critical the drop or increase is on whichever key performance indicator we're reporting?

Now, take the opposite tack. Reboot your reporting systems starting with the least necessary data. Ask yourself if it's understandable, proven, and reliable; and just as importantly, is it executable? You'll likely see that a lot of the numbers you're receiving are just plain useless. It's overload; it's a time drain, a brain drain; and it keeps you from being the most efficient operator you can be.

Many of you are drowning in data, and there's no need for that. You may need to shut it all down and start from scratch by simply asking the same question dealers asked themselves back when they first started selling cars—where are the consumer eyeballs today? Where are they looking for vehicles? Because that's where you need to be.

A lot of dealers have lost sight of some core fundamentals, because they have twenty vendors telling them twenty different things, each with their own agendas. Their message is driven by what they are capable of providing, not by what you need. If they were honest about it, they would just say, "Look at this vanity metric over here, that's really where your focus should be, because that's what we know how to deliver … even though ultimately it doesn't do much for your sales." They're all naturally jockeying for position. Many of our people started on the dealership side, and they say the same thing—*the data overload affects your ability to perceive the all-important basics of selling cars.* And it can be very difficult to identify who is actually legit and who's just telling you what you want to hear so that you'll cut them a check.

But an even bigger problem with relying on data alone is it can lead you to dangerous and false conclusions.

Here's a simple example. Let's say your financial advisor emails you to let you know your investment in a mutual fund is up 5 percent. *Wow,* you think, *that's great!* However, you shouldn't start partying just yet. Let's say, after you received that email, you then went and took a look at the major stock market indicators over the last few months and saw they were up 12 percent. Meaning you're actually down at least 7 percent from where you should be. Still pumping your fist in the air? Probably not. Because you just discovered that your fund is actually underperforming in a major way—and that's the *information* that really counts.

You probably aren't thrilled to be forced to think again about the COVID pandemic, but I bring it up here again because it also provides a cogent example of data versus information. The spread of the virus has been detailed through data disseminated on a daily basis, but the numbers themselves tell you only so much. For example, maybe you heard there were only ten cases in your area. And you might have let out another *Wow, that's great!* in response. But put off the partying once again because let's say you then discovered only one hundred out of the seven hundred and fifty thousand people that live in your area were actually tested. So who knows how many cases are actually out there? Probably thousands.

Now let's relate the issue of data versus information directly back to your business, your dealership. And let's say you just glanced at your online numbers and said to yourself, "Oh no. My website traffic is down, and my leads are down. We have to do something." Well, you're probably right—but what action? Numbers alone won't tell you what you need to do to regain ground.

Two KPIs are in play in this situation—website traffic and leads. But those numbers don't exist in a vacuum. If you have less inventory on hand, that could decrease those KPIs. If you've upped your prices, that could also be a factor. In other words, before you act, you have to analyze if anything significant has changed at your dealership or in the local economy that pushed those numbers down. You have to put those numbers in context. You have to derive information from not only the data but also any external issues that would directly or indirectly impact what's on the spreadsheet you're looking at.

We find that a lot of dealers might get a report from a vendor that is very specialized and in a silo. For example, they may just give you those raw website numbers I just talked about, along with their own judgments based on that data—but they may not have access to the *causes* behind any trends, be they positive or negative, that are in play. When that's the case, hit the pause button before you take any action they advocate. Because the numbers just can't tell you the whole story.

CONVERTING DATA INTO INFORMATION

> The big gap between data and information is *context*.

The big gap between data and information is *context*. That's provided by understanding all the variables surrounding the data and which are most relevant to whatever is being analyzed. Data is just an input, one of perhaps many, used to create meaningful information, which will provide you the bottom line of what's truly going on, as well as point you in the direction you should take next. Data, in contrast, doesn't take into consideration your goals or most other external factors. If someone told you that if you walked a mile north, you'd reach their house—well, that's data. If you then found out there was a lake between where you were and where their house was—meaning your "walk" would be largely underwater—that's information.

Let's go back to our example of the dealership website vendor. Let's say they charge X number of dollars to provide you with a website that features your inventory, facts about your dealership, a page that allows consumers to schedule service appointments, etc.—all the things you'd expect to find on a dealership website. You naturally want to hold this vendor accountable to making sure the site is working as well as possible and is generating a reasonable number of leads. For transparency's sake, the vendor sends you, on a monthly or even weekly basis, numbers representing categories like unique visitor traffic, variations from the last report, number of visits to individual pages, and so forth—data that's mostly just coming from Google Analytics or something similar. Which means it's standardized and industry agnostic.

Maybe that data tells you that the traffic to check out your used car inventory is down. You've had fewer unique visitors; the number has fallen by 3 percent. Well, that again is simply data. It doesn't tell me what I have to do to get the number back up, because I don't know what the *real* problem is—in other words, the *why* behind that number decreasing. That piece of data has to be converted into information.

Questions have to be asked. What influenced the used car traffic? Was it how much media you bought driving visitors to your used cars website page? How many used vehicles do you have in stock? Did the pricing change? Are the photos of the cars not as high quality as before for some reason? And context has to be accounted for. Let's say this traffic decrease happened near the beginning of the pandemic, when the future was a huge question mark. So maybe, because you were rattled, you cut back the used car inventory 50 percent in order to hoard cash. Keeping that in mind, when you see only a 3 percent drop as your used car stock was actually cut in half … is that a bad thing?

Suddenly, that doesn't seem like a loss. It seems like a win.

By the way, when the pandemic was beginning to gain steam, a lot of dealers were scrambling, simply because they, like the rest of us, had no idea what was going to happen. Not only were they seeing website traffic drop, but showroom visits plummeted. Or, in the case of a lockdown, there was no showroom availability at all. So many did pull back resources until they could see more clearly how things were going to shake out. All these variables and more were changing at once, and not in a good direction. The data showed it clearly. But was it *actionable*? No. Which is why PureCars, as well as other vendors, was enlisted to help determine how dealers should react to the sudden shifts in consumer behavior, because this was completely new territory for all of us.

So we did what we do, which is process the data into information. For example, how did our clients' drop in business compare to the competition's? To the market at large? If one of our clients had a smaller drop than similar dealerships, then we could let them know they were doing relatively okay, considering the situation.

The next question, however, was the really important one: What should the dealer do now to keep as much business as possible moving forward? Well, another effect of the pandemic was that Google AdWords was suddenly less expensive to use for advertising. To a lot of car dealers, that was catnip. One of the primary advertising platforms was suddenly a great deal, so naturally, most dealers thought it was time to take advantage of the discount and throw more money in that direction.

But here's the thing: the drop in AdWords pricing was just another piece of data. In other words, that alone wasn't enough to justify going "full Google." When you took a deeper dive into what was happening online, you could quickly determine that people who were on lockdown felt, with good reason, very isolated. That in turn stimulated activity on social media platforms, which skyrocketed. That meant you could generate a better ROI spending more on Facebook, despite the lower AdWords price.

Now that's valuable information.

The difference between data and information is something online giants like Google are finally waking up to. Google is now generating what they call "Data Shorts," which give invaluable context to the massive amounts of data they generate. For example, they've broken down such subject matter as how the pandemic has changed online activity between friends, what makes an advertising campaign automatically inclusive, and how businesses can use Google data to identify trends. (You can check these out and more on the Think with Google website, in the Data Shorts on Consumer Insights page). These Data Shorts literally convert data into information and enable you to see concrete examples of the result.

Relying on information rather than data empowers you to understand the *why* of the data. Once you gain that understanding of why the numbers are moving the way they are, once you have information that's reliable and actionable, you can execute to tackle the real variable that's affecting data. This process puts you in control and gives you the confidence to create positive change. And that translates into higher profits.

FLUID ADVERTISING

The most effective way to execute on information backed by data is through *fluid advertising*.

Let me explain fluid advertising by first telling you what it's not. It's not a billboard on the highway. It's not a radio or TV commercial you've been running forever. In other words, it's not traditional media. Digital marketing allows you to change things up quickly and pivot dramatically when you need to. You can change your target market, your online ad placement, your budget, your search terms, everything … and usually you can do all this very quickly and efficiently. Traditional media? Not so much.

Think of it this way. Let's say you have a friend you can only reach by mail for some reason. You send them a letter, and it takes, maybe, five days to arrive. But a few days after you send it, you discover you forgot to tell them something important. Well, now you have to write another letter, put it in an envelope, go out to the mailbox, and then wait another five days for them to get it. In contrast, if you were friends with that person online, you could message them instantly. And with many platforms, you would even know when that person looked at your message.

Traditional media is more like the friend you can only reach by mail. If you want to change a billboard … well, you have to create a whole new design and have the outdoor company print it out and put it up. That's expensive and it takes time. Same with a radio or TV buy. To change gears with a campaign, you actually have to go produce a new commercial and do a new buy. And in both cases, you basically have to be able to predict the future and try to guess what will work days and even weeks out. You never really get a good read on whether you're actually reaching the right audience. In other words, you can't get anywhere near an exact ROI for a specific campaign you've invested in.

Digital advertising provides you with a quicker and more fluid marketing capability and a method to get more accurate and timely results. You can then use those results to make your next moves more effective. If you suddenly get some new high-demand vehicles in stock, you can quickly tweak your online efforts to get the message out. On the right platform, it's easy to change things up, because digital is designed for easy revisions, as well as detailed tracking. You don't have to lose time and money waiting to deliver an important new marketing message. You know in real time how successful it is, whether it's working or whether you need to change the details on the fly. Just a few keystrokes will get the job done.

Yes, traditional media can raise your brand awareness. But I will say this: you probably already are close to the level of brand awareness you need. Most dealerships stay in place for a very long time, and manufacturers award very few new ones these days. You don't see ninety Toyota dealerships in the metro Detroit area for good reason—there aren't enough customers to keep them all afloat. The car companies keep a limited number of dealerships out there for good reason. Even if you are in an area that is "over pointed," trying to outshout your competition for name recognition is expensive. Why not outsmart them by investing your money where the customer who is ready to buy is really shopping? *Online.*

So odds are you're already more established than most businesses. Local consumers already know where you are and have an idea of what vehicles you sell. That means brand awareness isn't your big challenge. Generating traffic and converting it to sales is. And that's why we recommend dealers focus on fluid advertising that will enable them to act quickly and effectively with their marketing. We know what works. On behalf of our clients, we have bought hundreds of millions of dollars of media on Google, Bing, Facebook, and various other online platforms.

But …

We have yet to see a dealer "ring the bell," in terms of actually spending the amount we recommend on a specific media channel. Instead, they keep their budgets in other less effective areas.

Take a look at what your dealership's search impression share is. You probably don't see percentages in the nineties. However, you should. I believe you could even see 100 percent if you committed to executing on what we've learned are the best practices in digital. If you're actually bidding on all terms, you should be able to capture your actual market, because you're advertising in a limited geographic area.

In contrast, Amazon *does* ring the bell, every time. They fill their funnel with the lowest cost to first convert traffic, then they open the next gate and fill that bucket. Then the next gate and the next gate and so on, until they meet their target cost per unit sold.

Here's where we return to the idea of data versus information. If you're looking at the pure data (i.e., the number of dollars we might ask you to spend on a digital channel), you might say, "Hell no, that's too much money." But if you look at it from the standpoint of what information is relevant, which is that you stand to make a lot more if you increase the digital budget, then it makes incredible sense. What doesn't make sense is if you rely on a huge expensive billboard, just because you see it when you're driving to work. In your mind, the billboard is doing a lot of heavy lifting when it comes to your marketing. The reality is there isn't a tangible ad cost per unit sold associated with it. It's not motivating a specific customer looking for a specific vehicle. It's only about brand awareness, not about stimulating sales—especially if that billboard has been sitting there for quite a while and nobody even gives it a second thought while passing it, except for you.

SEEING PAST COST PER CLICK

Now, let's apply the data-versus-information paradigm to Cost Per Click (CPC).

If you're selling, let's say, a box of nails for a dollar, you obviously can't afford to pay a hefty CPC. However, if you're a personal injury lawyer and a lead could bring you a million dollars or so in a settlement, not only can you afford to pay a substantial CPC, but you *want* to—because your ROI is going to be spectacular if just one out of twenty leads turns out to be a strong one.

The data point of the dollar figure you're paying on a CPC means almost nothing by itself. It matters, but not as much as you think it might—because that figure is all by its lonesome, without any context about how many more dollars it could bring into your dealership.

Let's say the CPC of marketing a Chevy Silverado is three dollars. Too much? Well, let's say you have plenty of those trucks on your lot. Not only that, but maybe your dealership is getting a dealer cash incentive—for every Silverado you sell, Chevy will pay out an extra two thousand dollars. Suddenly, paying more for that CPC is a shrewd move. There's more money to be made, so why wouldn't you be willing to invest more in a high CPC? Yes, other dealers may be driving the price of that CPC up even higher for the same reason—they see a chance to boost profits significantly. Does that mean you should bail? Absolutely not. You still have more upside, your ROI potential is still amazing, so you want to stay in the game, not sit it out on the bench and watch all the other players score, because this is where your investment will get the biggest return.

Data points alone are not enough to justify taking a specific action—or not taking it. You can't make a valid decision just on a number, unless you understand what that number means in a specific context. We've found that a lot of dealers get paralyzed by data points. They don't know how to translate them into information that they can execute on. So you're either going to need someone on-site who grasps how to do that or a partner who can provide you with information you can trust.

How do you know you can trust information? Make sure it's transparent, in terms of the provider offering a full explanation and a set of real numbers that back up their conclusions. The data they're working from has to be fact-based. And the information itself has to be proven, understandable, reliable, and executable. (Yes, the acronym created from those four words spells *Pure*. And that's just how we decided what to call ourselves.)

LIFETIME VALUE

Data is especially problematic if it's siloed from other important data points.

For example, the revenue-generating departments of most dealerships are very fragmented. There's a parts manager, a service manager, a new car manager, a used car manager, and so on. So when you look at your financial reports, these categories are walled off from each other.

This wasn't that big a deal in the past. But now, as margin erosion continues, it becomes more and more of an issue. For most dealerships, the service department is more of a profit center than the showroom. It's like when movie theaters used to make their real money at their concession stands—the purported core business isn't where the most revenue is generated. Instead, car sales help bring more customers into the service department. Which means, suddenly, that the service department has to become top of the class in terms of both customer experience and revenue enhancement.

The brand that illustrates this idea, in my mind, is BMW. A new BMW vehicle comes with a three- or four-year maintenance plan included with the purchase price. And the net result of this incentive is the dealership enjoys incredible retention numbers postsale. People keep bringing their vehicles in there for service, and a recurring income stream is developed. These are customers that have a strong lifetime value, as I discussed earlier in this book, which, frankly, more and more represents the lifeblood of a car lot's sustainability. Yet, in all my years, I have never seen a public or a private dealer group report on lifetime value numbers—which is why I flagged it as a blind spot in chapter 1.

This again is another war between data and information. If you're paying a new car manager to write as much gross as possible with a sale, then that manager is going after a customer who will pay the highest price. That manager isn't going to consider if that customer lives within a reasonable distance that would motivate them to bring the car to that dealership for service. The manager's motivation is delivering the goals their boss sets for them.

This means everyone concerned may be chasing the wrong data point. If that manager would instead favor local customers and offer them better deals, the dealership would be better off in the long run because now the revenue they derive from that local customer isn't a one-off. They could, in fact, profit off that customer for years, simply by identifying the opportunity to deliver a surprisingly positive experience to the right customer.

Let's go further with this scenario. Let's say a dealer sold one hundred cars a year ago. Of those one hundred, let's suppose twenty were sold to nonlocal customers, because the dealer simply offered the best price, so it was worth the drive. It's highly likely only two of those one hundred came back in to service their vehicle. Short term, the dealer made a pot of money. Long term, the dealer lost a lot of potential future revenue. This happened because the potential lifetime value of those customers never occurred to anyone involved in the deal. If it had, perhaps a salesperson would have asked a prospective customer where they lived, and if it was close enough to the dealership, maybe the salesperson would have offered a better price, knowing there was a good chance the lifetime value of the customer would more than make up for the discount. It just makes sense to attract customers who have the highest probability of servicing with you because this can pay generational dividends for years and even decades to come.

A CRM tool or a dealer management system could most likely analyze just how much revenue lifetime value adds to the profitability level of a customer. But from a day-to-day standpoint, it's just not a consideration, and I think it absolutely should be. Dealers just aren't thinking about lifetime value as it relates to the allocation of their marketing dollars for customer acquisition. They're thinking more like that new car manager who just wants to move as many units as possible for as high a gross as possible.

Here's how to think of lifetime value from the standpoint of information rather than data. Let's assume that it costs you $500 to pull in someone from outside your market area to buy a vehicle from you. Now, let's say that according to your data, in your competitive backyard, it costs you $600 to get a new customer in the door. For a dealer looking only at the data, the conclusion would be to max out the opportunity outside your market as the cost per sale is less and margins benefit. But if we translate the deeper information, the more expensive customer to win will deliver exponentially more value over their ownership lifecycle, which would likely justify a more aggressive upfront investment to win their loyalty. There's simply no reason not to pay that higher marketing price tag and even get more bullish to win a higher share of the nearby market. That's viewing car sales from an informational point of view, rather than just a data-driven one.

And it can be done. As I've said, a dealer can easily own search terms, social news feeds, retargeting ads, and video delivery in their area if they pay the price. But none that I've encountered will say something like, "I don't care if it costs $90,000 this month, I want every customer in this area who is interested in our new or used vehicles to see our dealership everywhere, every time." It's never happened as far as I know.

A really good marketer should say, "How do I maximize my ad spend to have the highest return today AND the highest lifetime value in the future?" Why be shortsighted if you can be long-sighted? But this industry, and to be fair, many other industries as well, have siloed compensation plans that result in managers with specific goals that have left them and their salespeople in a box. They can't seem to break out of that box and see the forest for the trees, because nobody in the dealership training process or management hierarchy has ever taught or incentivized them to consider the potential lifetime value of each customer they encounter. All too often, an internet director finds it hard to say, "Boss, last month I spent $10,000 more on advertising and my cost per unit sold increased, but our cost per lead came down 22 percent, and this month we're seeing cost per sale drop by 35 percent." Because there's too high a chance that the manager would react with an irritated frown and a barrage of questions—"Why did you have to spend more? What happened? Go cancel something before this gets out of control." What they should be doing is smiling at the extra revenue generated and complimenting the manager on a job well done. I know this is "tough talk," but I'm just suggesting you take a moment and think about where you stand on this issue. Shifting to the right viewpoint can have a big impact on your business.

So think about how you might analyze lifetime value data and make it a part of your daily process. How can you do that? First, you can pull reporting from the service department that shows you where your service customers live. Then you want to know how many of those customers bought from you, and you want to overlay that data. Next, you can look at the areas where the highest percentage of customers who bought vehicles returned to your dealership for service. You can analyze your profits from that set of customers to see how much money that meant to your balance sheet. And by the way, don't stop at this macro level. Now you can look at the results based on model, price point, and some other data slices to really maximize the marketing strategy.

The next thing you might want to do is look at your ad costs for the target area. Should you spend more in that area if the cost of marketing is more expensive? Well, if the value is there, if 70 percent of the customers in that area return for service for at least the next three years and generate another $900 or even $1900 in gross profit per customer, well, the answer is absolutely.

Going after customers with potential lifetime value is absolutely a great move to make. If you looked behind the curtain with a private equity group or a venture capitalist looking at a business, they would ask, "What's the customer acquisition cost?" And let's say, to dumb down the numbers, it's $10. The next question would be, "What's a customer's average lifetime value?" If it's, say, only $5, that's likely a big problem moving forward. It's obviously far more lucrative to acquire a customer for $10, and have that customer end up making you $100 over time.

Dealerships gravitate toward KPIs. They're very competitive and successful because of their drive to continuously improve. But to us, you really want to be focused on acquisition costs. You want to be focused on lifetime value. To maximize profitability in the short term as well as the long term, we suggest you look deeper. If you really want to be focused on acquisition costs, be sure to convert your data into information. You want to be focused on lifetime value because that's where you maximize your opportunities.

***

Data versus information. It's really a one-sided fight, because data points have blinders on. Solid information is meant to provide as close to a 360-degree view as possible and deliver it in ways that are immediately actionable. The smartest people I know are those who compile a tremendous amount of relevant data, which they then analyze, connect, and present as understandable information that they can execute on. And if an organization can then orchestrate their information to deliver executable insights to each key manager in the business to help them make better decisions in real time? That's where the magic happens.

Knowing that, are you willing to buck what you've always done and even what your gut may be telling you to do? Are you willing instead to commit to moving forward on actionable information that may take you in totally new marketing directions? I would love to see you examine a few of the strategies we've laid out in this chapter and try them if you haven't before now. Do it for a few months—commit to following not just the data but the information that emerges from it. See if you realize better results.

This has been a real game changer for many dealers … and it could be for you.

REFLECTION EXERCISES

1. Think about what you rely heaviest on for your decision-making, data or information. If the answer is data, think about how you can connect the dots to transform that data into information.

2. How much of your marketing budget is devoted to fluid advertising? Is the majority of dollars still dedicated to traditional media? How can you switch it up?

3. Think about the steps you'd want to take in order to roll lifetime value as an important factor in your customer acquisition efforts. Discuss those steps with the rest of management, and implement a plan to make it happen.

CHAPTER FOUR

BREAKING THROUGH THE BUDGET BOX

If you chose not to grow, you're staying in a small box with a small mindset. People who win go outside of that box.
—KEVIN HART

I was talking with a large Chevrolet dealer in Kentucky in October of last year. He wanted my input because he was planning his marketing budget for the following year. Although that's not an unusual process for a dealer, it still blew my mind. How can you commit yourself to numbers for an entire year unless you're Nostradamus? You can't possibly know what's going to be happening in the marketplace twelve months out.

My mind was flooded with questions about this dealer's operation. How much will they need to market certain cars? What's their price to market going to be? What are dealer and factory incentives going to be? He couldn't know the answers to those questions and a whole lot of others while he was locking in that budget. To go to that high level and start assigning dollar amounts to media channels when you're in the dark like that ... well, it doesn't pay dividends.

Look, I get it. This is actually how most businesses still handle marketing; they budget way in advance. But it's the twenty-first century, and that viewpoint doesn't help you make money the way it used to. I've already pointed out in this book that a fixed budget can actually cost you money, and now, let me prove it to you again. As I'm writing this book, the NADA average of the advertising cost per sale is around 640 bucks.[7] At the same time, there is a large US public dealer group that has a much lower ad cost per sale—$100.

Yes, that's five times less.

Why the huge difference? Because the public dealer group finally saw their way past one of the biggest dealer blind spots—they removed the "muscle memory" around marketing budgets. They're working with what's effective now, as opposed to what was effective twenty years ago. The most profitable and effective ways of selling vehicles have radically changed in the past few years. Of selling *anything*, really. And that requires a big mindset shift from anyone who's been in the car business for a number of years.

I made that shift myself with my very first small e-commerce business in the early 2000s. My father was a CPA, so he wanted to help guide me with the financial ins and outs of what I was doing. He would ask me, "What's your ad budget? Your business relies on advertising." My answer? "I don't have a budget." He didn't like hearing that. He told me point blank, "Your business is going to fail. You have to have a budget."

---

7   NADADATA2019, https://www.nada.org/WorkArea/DownloadAsset. aspx?id=21474861098.

I responded with what is now the essence of our marketing philosophy:

"I don't need a budget if I have a part with an $80 margin. I can acquire a customer for about $6, and I know anything over $50 of profit for that product meets my threshold. And I'm going to keep spending until I hit that equilibrium point where the next incremental dollar is negative effect."

Which is exactly what the e-commerce giants do right now.

We're going to get into more detail on how important the cost per sale number should be to your overall marketing strategy in the next chapter. But first, let's downshift in this chapter and look back at what traditional car marketing used to look like—and what today's marketplace now requires.

A NEW KIND OF BUDGET

Newspapers have been around since the 1600s and billboards have been around since the 1800s. And unfortunately, this is where a great deal of car advertising remains—in traditional media. Then radio and TV came of age in the 1900s, along with direct mail and other print outlets. These were all mediums where creative had to be designed and executed in advance—usually by an ad agency—and booked in advance. Dealers would lay out their budgets for the year, just like the dealer in Kentucky I chatted with, and add extra money for those special times of year when they would want to be particularly aggressive (holidays, the release of new models, etc.).

How many sales could be attributed to those modes of traditional advertising? Almost impossible to measure and almost always anecdotal in nature. A customer saying, "Hey, I saw your billboard!"

or "Hilarious TV spot!" would make a dealer think that particular placement was a winner. And even though that piece of feedback might have you jumping for joy, that's just one person, and it reflects only that one person's experience.

Something we hear from a lot of dealers is this: "At least half of my ad budget is effective … I'm just not sure which half." That rings the bell for me, because you just can't effectively calculate the ROI of most of these marketing efforts, at least not in time to make the kind of strategic moves that enable you to maximize your revenue. So you spend more than you need to, simply because you want to make sure you cover all the bases.

With digital, you don't have to cover all the bases. You don't have to pay $500 in marketing to sell a car. You can get a lot closer to the $100 figure, because the data tells you which bases (i.e., which channels) are worth the money and effort. You can learn quickly which channels deliver the best results. You know exactly what online ads draw clicks and which convert the best. It's not a subjective process, like traditional media, where you could take much of the money you spend, stuff it in a sack, and toss it in the garbage for all the impact it had.

Digital, in contrast, is completely evidence-based, which makes it infinitely more efficient and cost effective. Best of all, it's *targeted*. You can go for the specific prospects you want for a specific vehicle. And because it's still a relatively young medium, digital marketing continues to be more precise, more nimble, and much more powerful.

Meanwhile, the power of traditional media continues to be diluted and weakened by a growing number of alternative choices. People don't read newspapers (at least the printed kind) very much anymore. Physical circulation numbers have fallen to levels from

1940,[8] when we had about a third of the population we have now. People also barely listen to commercial radio anymore; they listen to podcasts and satellite radio. As for TV, traditional buying tactics are quickly eroding and giving way to a new world of digitally targeted TV ads delivered via smart TVs, Roku boxes, Amazon Fire Sticks, and Apple TV. And again, your customers aren't using traditional media to determine where to buy the car they want. They're going on their smartphones and tablets not just to pass the time but also to research products they want to buy. In just one decade, according to the Wharton School, the daily amount of time Americans spend with digital media has doubled from three hours a day to six hours a day.[9]

So is there still a place for traditional media? Yes. If you are one of the few dealers in America that's either new to the market or just moved locations. These are both very unlikely scenarios these days, but if that's your situation, then I can easily understand why you're blasting TV and radio ads to come see my new, say, Mercedes store. But if you already have an established twenty-plus-million-dollar facility, and you're in a geographic area that both you and your manufacturer believe is the right location for the kinds of vehicles you're selling, you probably don't need to talk too much about where you are. Instead, you can spend your money talking about what you have and directing that talk strategically through the media channels where you can target your most likely customers. You can't be as strategic as you want to be, however, if you still insist on creating a yearlong marketing budget in advance. In these times, it just doesn't make sense. *When you lock in those numbers, you're*

---

8   "Newspapers Fact Sheet," Pew Research Center, July 2019, https://www.journal-ism.org/fact-sheet/newspapers/.

9   "Digital Versus Traditional Marketing: What Today's C-Suite Needs to Know," Wharton Online, https://online.wharton.upenn.edu/blog/digital-versus-traditional-marketing/.

handcuffing yourself. Suddenly, you can't react and pivot when you should—causing you to miss out opportunities and more profits.

Let's assume your dealership gets a large percentage of their used cars from trade. Can you predict what cars you'll get in on trade next month and how much demand there will be for them? No. You can assume the used car manager will, of course, pay less for a car that's some dog that's not desirable and pay more for a car that will fly off the lot in no time. The throttle of increase and decreased dollars based on demand of that unit will happen. That's the used car manager's job.

But that's exactly how you want to handle your marketing. You want to be able to use that same throttle to increase or decrease digital dollars depending on what you're trying to sell. That dog of a car? You probably need to increase digital dollars (if it will work). The one that will fly off the lot? You can decrease or not spend at all if it's likely to sell on its own.

So you want to leave yourself room to change gears and reallocate marketing dollars when necessary. And it will be necessary. In 2020, the year the dealer from Kentucky was budgeting for, the pandemic hit and of course, that turned everything upside down. And I'm sure all that careful budgeting got thrown out the window. Nobody knew how COVID-19 would affect the car industry. It turned out it propelled used car demand through the roof—something no one could have seen coming and a trend that should have motivated dealers to readjust their marketing. While it's true that in most years, you won't face that kind of dramatic change, there are always variations and cycles you can be poised to take advantage of *if you permit your marketing budget to be fluid.*

THE E-COMMERCE MINDSET

The best budgeting model dealers can replicate is that of e-commerce. In e-commerce, analysts are constantly looking at the data and converting it into hard information they can act on.

You should also be looking at all the indicators surrounding your current inventory so you can know with a high level of probability what vehicles will sell on their own, which need merchandising attention, and which simply need a visibility boost from advertising. Then, look at how you can maximize the sale rate and your profit margin by leveraging a nimble media mix across channels and optimize it for a lower cost per sale. That's the thinking behind strong e-commerce. Amazon does not set fixed marketing budgets. *They think in terms of what they can earn, not in terms of what they have to spend.* What a dealer has to add to the equation is the cost per sale as a percentage of profit. A fully loaded GMC Denali is obviously going to generate more profit than a base subcompact, so it's worth upping the cost per sale as far as your target net margin allows.

Now, dealing with all these constant ongoing calculations and variations may seem overwhelming, but consider this: it probably shouldn't be *you* who's dealing with it. If you agree with the fundamental philosophy that a car dealership should have a heavy digital marketing footprint, then you should align with someone who will help you make that transition, whether it's through an outside provider, an in-house department, business intelligence software, or some mix of the three. You need an expert who knows how to track the data and interpret it to get useful information so you can see at a glance what's working and what's not and, based on that information, double down on successes and draw down on low return investments.

Most of the car industry understands the shift to online marketing is necessary, because … well, consumers are overwhelmingly focused on that space. And all dealers are making that shift at one level or another. NADA's latest statistics on dealer ad spending by medium illustrates the continued decline of traditional advertising and the rise of digital—56 percent of dealership ad spending went to internet advertising, followed by TV (17.6 percent), radio (10.1 percent), direct mail (6.9 percent), and newspaper (6 percent).[10]

There's a host of additional reasons this shift is happening; digital is cheaper, faster, more targeted, and easily trackable. But dealers who take an e-commerce approach to fixed and variable ops enjoy an overwhelming competitive advantage. Just throwing your ad spend to digital does NOT guarantee success. For example, the dealers who spend only $100+ to sell a vehicle versus the dealers who spend around $500 maximize the flexibility and speed with which they can change up their digital plans by making information-driven decisions on a daily basis.

> The dealers with the lowest ad cost per unit sold dedicate a whopping 95 percent of their budget to digital.

They also commit more resources to digital. I just quoted the latest NADA figure available for how dealers spend their marketing dollars. Digital accounted for 56 percent. You might think that's a lot, but to me, it's not nearly enough *because the dealers with the lowest ad cost per unit sold dedicate a whopping 95 percent of their budget to digital.* Again, they have the mindset that focuses on goals,

---

10 "Dealer Advertising 2020: Less Traditional, More Social, Local Interactions," Dealer News Today, January 17, 2020, https://www.dealernews-today.com/dealer-advertising-2020-less-traditional-more-social-local-interactions/#:~:text=Even%20with%20varying%20aspects%20of,on%20average%2C%20%24625%20in%202018.

not budgets. It's about how much they can make, not about how much the budget allows them to spend in order to achieve their unit sales. They're not saying, "Let's be careful about our budget. We don't want to overspend." The smart dealer says, "I don't know what my budget's going to be this month, but I know what I need to market and where to do it, and I can effectively predict within a reasonable range what my ROI will be on each dollar I invest."

WHY SOME DEALERS ARE RESISTANT TO CHANGE

It's hard to deny a predominately digital strategy makes incredible sense on paper. But it takes a while for businesses who are set in their ways to make this kind of change. This isn't unique to the car business. For example, the vast majority of community banks still tag less than 20 percent of their marketing budgets to digital,[11] which is frankly amazing to me.

There are three contributing factors I would point to for continuing resistance in many dealerships to embracing an all-in digital strategy.

AD AGENCIES

In general, media for dealership advertising has historically been bought by ad agencies. Ad agencies charged a monthly fee for providing creative, and then they made most of their money on the margin they raked in between the buy and the sell price of the media. So if you as their client buy $40,000 on TV ads and their contract

---

11 Mark Gibson, "Your 2020 Marketing Spend: Digital vs. Traditional," ABA Bank Marketing, January 22, 2020, https://bankingjournal.aba.com/2020/01/your-2020-marketing-spend-digital-vs-traditional/.

gives them 15 percent of that buy, they just made $6,000. So those agencies are more motivated to get the dealer to commit to a fixed traditional media budget to protect against revenue erosion throughout the year; that's how they make and protect their bank. They make a lot more on media buys than on creative, so if a tactic in the media buy isn't working, they often persuade the dealership to spend more … even if it's in areas where maybe they shouldn't.

THE FIXED-BUDGET MINDSET

The other problem is the fixed-budget mindset we've already spoken of. When a dealer asks us, "What do you think I'm going to make this year in profit?" we can't really make that prediction. So they create a budget based on what they think they can afford and give us a limited pool of money to work with. And again, when we spot an opportunity that would require going beyond that amount, the decision maker at the dealership often isn't willing to go beyond what they budgeted— even if it's very likely to make them more than enough revenue and profit to make up for it.

A VENDOR FOR EVERY CHANNEL

In the past, media buys were split between vendors. The radio rep sold radio. The TV rep sold TV. The newspaper rep sold … well, you can see where I'm going with this. Anyway, seven years ago, we did much the same thing. We sold Google. We sold paid search. And so forth. Under this system, there really wasn't an easy way for someone to have access to all relevant digital media channels through one provider. Generally, you had a bunch of them all fighting for the channels they individually sold, because that was where their bread and butter was.

Six years ago, we decided to change all that at PureCars. We made large scale investments in order to become the first automotive digital marketing platform to offer dealers everything they need to compete and thrive in their markets in a single solution—a solution that enables full funnel, integrated advertising across all major digital channels, dealer website conversion tools, and powerful business intelligence features. We don't favor one digital methodology over another unless it's justified by the data. Instead, we want to choose what will work most effectively for our client, because that's the right thing to do. We use machine learning components to analyze data and turn it into actionable information (see the previous chapter for more on that process). From those results, we might learn, Hey, Facebook has a higher success rate in selling a certain make of car. Meaning if we're talking about a Honda dealer, we may move a lion's share of their budget into Facebook from other channels until we max out the efficiency on their cost per sale. If we strike gold, we follow the vein as far as it takes us. We work hard to eliminate any media bias on our side, because we want results to dictate what wins the next round of our clients' marketing dollars.

With all this in play, in three to five years, almost all dealers will likely not function on a fixed budget. Because otherwise, they won't be able to compete effectively against those dealers who are optimizing to daily business outcomes. Instead, they need to monitor what's going on with all the digital channels and, on an ongoing basis, determine how much they can make per channel on each model. The e-commerce mindset has to be in place to make the most of that marketing strategy, a mindset that focuses on a micro level in real time about how to achieve the cheapest marketing cost per sale while driving the most sales. That mindset should also treat each vehicle as a unique product, with an assessment based on size of the market demand and the maximum potential profit margin. Most dealers are going to end up with that mindset someday, simply because it will be necessary. The question is, will you be one of the ones that end up changing because everyone else did, or will you be the one in your market that leads the charge and wins the day?

Yes, disruption can be hard to embrace. But we must accept that disruption *has already happened.* The dealerships that are running the most efficient and goal-oriented marketing are the ones who are using analytics and A/B testing and hiring vendors or platforms that have the agility to change direction quickly. They're leading the way in lower marketing costs and higher results. *And they're also able to lower the asking prices on many of their vehicles, win more sales online, while making more money.*

How? Keep reading.

THE "DIGITAL DISCOUNT"

Here's one more potentially huge benefit of lowering your marketing cost per sale. Let's say, by handling your budget in the way I'm advocating, you bring that figure down a few hundred dollars per vehicle. You can stick that money in your pocket and whistle a happy tune— or you can apply part of that saved money to increasing market share.

Let's start with a proposition that's just common sense: if you price a vehicle grossly under market, it will sell with way less marketing firepower than a vehicle that is priced over market. Look, you can always find someone to buy an overpriced car, but the problem is, what will it take to make that happen? Do you have to pay to funnel ten thousand people to your website before someone bites? On the other hand, let's say you discount that car by accessing the money you saved on marketing. If you price the vehicle correctly, you might have 150 calls about it within an hour.

Think about it. If the average dealer has a $500 ad cost and you can get it down to $100, you could say, "Well, I can either put that $400 into my profits, or I can take half or even two-thirds of that margin and lower prices and close more business and make more profit. If the competition is still spending $500 per car to make a sale, they can't match my price." By doing that, you're creating a flywheel that begins to spin faster and faster, until it's really hard to slow it down. I mean, let's face it, the dealers that are the biggest in their markets don't have the highest prices. They're the ones offering the best deals. And manipulating your marketing dollars in this way allows you to be that dealer. You're the one who's actually got those "low, low prices" every other lot in town is claiming to have.

Suddenly, you're building the kind of momentum that makes it hard for the other guys to catch up with you. They'll have their excuses. They might say, "I can't compete with the dealer group. They have efficiency. They have more scale. They have more people." But that's not the whole story. The digital technology is what's really enabling them to thrive. And every dollar they end up saving, they put either toward profits or toward lowering the asking prices on vehicles. The secret sauce is in finding the equilibrium between maximizing profit and creating the lowest cost per sale, which drives velocity, profitability, and competitive advantage.

If I were to sum up how I view effective marketing budgeting, I would make this the bottom line: *it's all about being goal-oriented, rather than budget-oriented.* If you look at a custom F-150 and say, "Well, I can make $6,000 on a sale. But it's going to cost me double my normal marketing dollars. However, that $6,000 represents six times my normal profit. Hell, that's a great investment." That, in my view, is what smart marketing is all about. It's employing a dynamic budget process that allows you to spend more when you can make more and hold back when you don't need to prime the pump on an already in-demand vehicle.

That dynamic process should be built around the cost per sale strategy. In the next chapter, I'll reveal how to put that strategy into action.

REFLECTION EXERCISES

1. How do you think about your style of marketing? Are you adapting to an e-commerce model or not?

2. Do you have different vendors handling different marketing channels for your dealership? Does this cause conflicts? Would it be easier to hand over all the reins to the same agency?

3. How big a part does traditional media play in your marketing budgeting? Could changing up the mix improve your results? Discuss with your current vendor to get their take on it.

CHAPTER FIVE

THE COST PER SALE STRATEGY

KNOWING WHAT TO MARKET AND WHEN

In the end, all business operations can be reduced to three words: people, product, and profits.
—LEE IACOCCA

C huck Hutton Toyota in Memphis, Tennessee, had a problem. Coming into 2020, the dealership's marketing department had put a heavy focus on new inventory—100 percent of its paid search budget went to new cars. Historically, as a Toyota dealer in a metro area, that approach made sense. They had low funnel traffic in paid search and enough new car volume to hit objectives, and everything was, you might say, motoring right along …

Then came the pandemic. Suddenly, the transit trucks were starting to show up half-empty … if they showed up at all. Suddenly, that strategy that made perfect sense a few weeks before hit a dead end. Suddenly, the dealership didn't have that new car volume it expected, because constraints were put on the new inventory.

Mitch James, sales manager at the dealership, talked to us about the massive challenge they suddenly faced.

"When we first got wind, I guess probably early March or mid-March, that the plants were going to shut down, the management team started looking at our new car inventory. Then, when Toyota announced that the plants were also going to be closed in April, we realized this was going to get really serious: we were going to run out of Camrys and Corollas by the end of May or early June. And we did get down to one or two, as well as just one Rav4 and one or two Tacomas.

"Luckily, we had the foresight to say, 'Hey, what are we going to do?' The answer was used cars. We started stocking up our used car inventory and went from between 75 and 80 used cars to 130, 140, 150 used cars."

Now, the next question was the best way to sell those used cars.

On our side, we saw that Facebook's daily user numbers had skyrocketed; they were up double digits since March. Marketing on that platform was cheap and the most cost-effective medium to flip the script and focus on Hutton's bulked-up used car inventory instead of the new models. So the management pulled 40 percent of those paid search dollars—why market cars you don't have in stock?—and instead, invested those dollars in Facebook ads.

The result? Suddenly Chuck Hutton Toyota was *killing* it. By June, they were breaking their all-time sales and profitability records, notching incredible numbers:

- Their revenue skyrocketed 339 percent.

- Their ROAS (Return on Advertising Spend) went up by 849 percent.

- *And they reduced their average marketing cost per sale by 32 percent.*

While other dealers were being dragged down by the new pandemic normal, Chuck Hutton Toyota was hitting new heights—because the dealership was willing to shift gears and aggressively market their used car inventory.

Mitch James says of the outcome, "Our numbers are through the roof. We're going to finish number two in the Cincinnati region in certified used cars for 2020, and we came out of nowhere to hit that goal. We were never even on the radar. And we're going to go hard and heavy for number one next year—because we made number two even though we weren't really marketing used cars much in January or February and through the middle of March.

"Twenty nineteen was a fantastic year. It was a record setting-year, but in 2020, we're going to blow 2019 out of the water."

Just as importantly, the dealership saw the great upside of pursuing a cost per sale marketing strategy. Hopefully, this chapter will do the same for you.

WHERE'S YOUR DIGITAL FOCUS?

Amazon, the world's largest online retailer. Carvana, the largest retailer in cars. The top performing dealerships in the country. All of these peak performers have one thing in common—their marketing strategy is all about achieving the lowest marketing cost per sale.

Each of these companies has given serious thought to what they're willing to spend to acquire a sale. Each rejects a fixed budget, which will inevitably be too tight (capped, even though there's still more demand out there) or too bloated (doling out marketing dollars inefficiently because that was "the plan"). These companies spend across various efficient marketing channels until they hit their maximum cost per sale. They spend dollars tactically depending on where consumer demand is the highest. And each employs fluid advertising in order to achieve their goals.

In the last chapter, we talked about breaking out of the traditional "budget box" in order to utilize fluid advertising that can react quickly to changing circumstances. The Chuck Hutton Toyota case study shows you the rewards you can reap from that kind of ability. You would be hard pressed to find a more dramatic example of changing circumstances than a pandemic shutting down a great deal of the country.

Digital marketing is obviously all about being nimble and fluid. It enables you to turn on a dime when it's required. Better still, it offers an unlimited array of options for you to choose from to overpower your competition. It's fun to pick the options you want when it comes to buying a car, but with digital, it can be hard to determine what options you need and what you don't if you're not an expert in the field. That's why, in the first chapter of this book, we identified one of our dealer blind spots as digital marketing being "a whole new world" for most shops. It's easy to get overwhelmed, especially when vendors are shoving shiny new objects at you every day. I imagine these are the kinds of pitches you frequently hear:

> Digital marketing is obviously all about being nimble and fluid.

- "Look at our Trends Report!"

- "Look at our Digital Retailing Tool!"

- "We have Penny Perfect Payments for your website!"

- "You need automated 360-degree videos for every car!"

- "Look at our AI and Machine Learning!"

- "Look at our ability to show you where shoppers live on Google Maps!"

It can be exhausting. How can you know what to trust when it comes to your marketing dollars? That's why many dealers revert back to that dangerous muscle-memory blind spot once again, over and over. They do what they've always done and fall back into the habit. But if we change nothing, nothing changes. And with margins continuing to erode, this is the time we must change.

There is another way to strip this overloaded arena down, and that's to just stick to a basic digital strategy and build on it. And the one we've found to be clearly the most powerful is the cost per sale strategy. You lower marketing costs and, at the same time, boost sales. There's beauty and simplicity in that idea.

However, it may seem too complex and convoluted to carry it out. After all, you have to constantly analyze the market and continually change up your marketing as a result. But the truth is experts know how to make this happen. We do it for thousands of clients today, including hundreds of single-point dealers, publicly traded auto groups, and tier-two associations, as well as agencies and OEMs.

But again, this strategy requires fluid advertising that's easy to adjust on the fly to sell specific cars. While the Chuck Hutton Toyota example represents a big category switch—from marketing primarily new vehicle inventory to marketing used inventory—what I hope you will take away from it is the fact that not only was the shop able to quickly shift gears in a major way with its marketing, but it was also able to prosper like never before, simply because it dramatically lowered its marketing cost per vehicle sold. And you can ramp up this philosophy to market specific vehicles, right down to the VIN number. As you obviously know, combining lower marketing costs and a marked increase in sales is as big a win-win as you can have at your dealership.

In contrast, let's get into our Wayback Machines (I don't know about you, but I always have mine charged and ready to go) and travel back to 1990, when digital marketing was barely a blip on the horizon. If the pandemic had hit then, Chuck Hutton Toyota would have had a helluva harder time making the pivot it accomplished in early 2020 with the traditional media options available at the time. They certainly couldn't have done it as fast. And some of the options, like outdoor, wouldn't have worked at all—it would require too much time and too much expense to pull off.

In other words, it was difficult to impossible, and more toward the impossible side, to use a cost per sale strategy. Targeting specific audiences with specific vehicles just couldn't be done back then— whereas that's the most powerful tactic we use today at PureCars on behalf of our clients.

Luckily, now every dealership can put that tactic into play if they want. And that makes it more important than ever to determine which vehicles you want to be marketing and how. The ability to micro-target and market a specific car or truck is available to all dealers. Why wouldn't you want to take advantage of that ability? Even dealership leaders can stretch their advantage that way.

PUTTING THE PEDAL TO THE METAL: SPEEDING UP MARKETING DECISIONS

When it comes down to determining which vehicles to market, the criteria you might have used in 1990 is still surprisingly relevant today, because even though the marketing landscape has radically changed, the fundamental principles of supply and demand still apply. That's why at PureCars, we first seek to explore with a client what vehicles are in demand and if they are stocked appropriately to fulfill the demand. We then look at merchandising to assess the dealer's competitive position in the market and identify if pricing or staging of the inventory is throttling velocity. We nail that down by looking at traffic to the dealership's site and checking out purchase cues. Are there a lot of prospects eyeing the dealer's inventory online? Are they digging further into the highlights on specific vehicles? Are there fail points where the shoppers are dropping out at a high rate? Are there operational breakdowns that are losing customers after they've engaged the dealership?

After we've assessed the competitive readiness of the store, we then turn to efficiencies. The average number of days it takes a model to sell is a big factor. If that number is, say, ten, that means the car is in high demand and the dealer is selling them faster than they can pull the plastic off them. These high-demand vehicles generally don't need to be marketed aggressively, because they're essentially selling themselves. Unfortunately, a lot of dealerships and even many tech providers don't recognize that fact. They're not seeing how consumers are doing crazy high numbers of Google searches to track these models down, which means they are, in fact, doing your work for you. Those cars will probably still sell within ten days, whether you spend $25,000 on advertising them or nothing at all. So why drain your ad budget when you don't need to? As long as you're doing good merchandising, the demand will finish the job for you. And that demand could obliterate your stock in no time, which means again … why throw money at marketing it?

(One big caveat: Dealers should benchmark their sales figures against the market as a whole. If that super-hot car isn't selling as well for you as it is for other dealerships, then it might need a boost, especially if you have a good supply to sell).

On the other hand, you might have a vehicle that's not moving off the lot in the time it should for whatever reason. In that case, you'll want to go hard on upping your merchandising with better photos and descriptions, as well as more marketing dollars—even an expanded geographic footprint. Although you're spending more than maybe you should to market that car, it's evened out by not spending as much (or anything) on the in-demand vehicle.

The bottom line of knowing which vehicles to market is this: it allows you to keep your average marketing cost per sale as low as possible. With digital, it's easy to do that. You can continually adjust what you're spending on which vehicles in order to keep overall cost down and your profits up.

> Knowing which vehicles to market allows you to keep your average marketing cost per sale as low as possible.

Let's take another trip in the Wayback Machine back to 1990. That's when newspapers were still a vital cog in the vehicle marketing machinery. Back then, a newspaper sales rep might walk into a dealership on a Thursday and ask, "What do you guys want to put in the Sunday full-page spread you bought?" The general manager would first check out the list of used vehicles on the lot, from the ones that have been on the lot the longest to the ones that have only been there a short period of time. The general manager would then say to the newspaper rep,

"Hey, this car has been sitting out there on the lot for ninety-one days. It needs to go. Let's slash the price by two grand and go big with that. I've got fifteen program cars I can beat the market price on by $1,500, so let's drop those in as well." They might then repeat that process with five or ten other vehicles that have also lingered too long.

Then the conversation might turn to the new car inventory. The GM might look at what he was being offered from the manufacturer in terms of dealer cash and other incentives, and say, "Okay, this is good. The Expeditions have a $7,000-off rebate if you have a military discount and you're a repeat customer. I've got thirty on the lot, and the new ones are coming out in just two months. Maybe I can max out my dealer cash."

In terms of determining what vehicles to market, that kind of logic hasn't changed. What has changed is the speed of the decision-making needed to take full advantage of the cost per sale strategy. *You just need to do it much quicker because your flow of inventory is moving faster than a once-a-week decision can optimize.* Not only that, but you need to apply this science to *all* your vehicles, not just the ones you can fit into the limitations of a newspaper ad. It's the e-commerce mindset I discussed in the last chapter.

It really is no longer operationally efficient to have a monthly marketing meeting and try to make decisions about what you're going to do over the next four weeks. With the complexity of inventory and market fluctuation, you need technology surfacing signals to make smarter decisions literally on a daily and hourly basis.

Think about the speed of e-commerce. Even though the consumer may still show up at the dealership to actually make a purchase, their process and their journey to that purchase is happening online. So a dealer has to function in a fashion similar to how an online retailer would by taking in real-time signals to determine what the right inventory to market is today or even in the next hour, based on the fluctuation of market supply, demand, pricing, merchandising, and what they have in stock to sell.

Here are a few foundational truths today's car dealers should focus on to absorb the kind of e-commerce mindset that's necessary today:

- **Projecting sales volumes a year—or even a month—in advance is an exercise in futility.** 2020 is the ultimate example of how external disruption can turn things upside down in a completely unexpected way. And it may have changed the way dealers do business forever by lowering on-the-lot inventory and selling more on-demand vehicles.

- **Instead of trying to read a crystal ball, read the room.** When you track what's happening in the marketplace at the moment and act strategically on that movement, you're going to realize much better results than you would by looking in the rearview mirror. The past is not a great predictor of the future.

- **Marketing dollars should be allocated based on what you have to sell, what you need to sell, and what channels are most effective to generate demand.** If you look back at the Chuck Hutton Toyota case study, the dealership had to pivot from new inventory to used. Selling used cars was suddenly an immediate priority. At the same time, Facebook's spike in traffic made that social media platform an attractive and cost-effective way to target the most likely buyers. It was a perfect opportunity.

- **You need advertising partners who can reliably guide you.** The right provider will not only have insight into hundreds of thousands of data points daily but will also have the tools to quickly turn data into information that will inform the recalibration of campaigns. They also won't (or shouldn't) have any bias toward any particular channel and will steer you to just the one that will provide the most bang for your buck.

SWITCHING CHANNELS

One of the key principles underpinning the cost per sale strategy is to uncover the most cost-effective and targeted marketing channels to sell your inventory. And I'd like to provide you with a great example of that to close this chapter out.

Let's step back again to traditional media for a moment—specifically television. TV commercials have always been attractive for businesses seeking to get the most eyeballs for their marketing message. Everyone used to watch conventional TV, so back in the day, you had a pretty good shot at reaching your potential customers. The problem was (and is) that you ended up with quantity, instead of quality, in terms of an audience. The vast majority of viewers weren't interested in buying a car at the moment. But the marketer was making an expensive bet that they could reach *enough* potential buyers to make the price of the commercial worth it.

Unfortunately, that bet simply doesn't pay off anymore.

Just as it has with most industries, the internet has completely disrupted the television experience—through Over-the-Top (OTT) video service subscriptions. I'm talking Netflix; I'm talking YouTube; I'm talking Hulu, Amazon Prime Video, IMDb-TV, Sling TV, Disney+, Peacock, and many more, because a multitude of powerful new OTT services popped up just in 2020 alone. All these platforms share one thing in common—consumers can use their internet connections to watch them without going through the satellite or cable TV companies. Before OTT, satellite and cable dominated. Viewers were forced to buy packages of channels, many of which they didn't even watch, because it was a monopolistic situation—if you wanted to watch TV, you needed DirectTV or Dish or Spectrum or whoever was supplying service in your area.

That was then; this is now. As of March 2020, OTT video subscriptions had raced past the traditional pay TV services. Parks Associates surveyed ten thousand US broadband households and discovered that 76 percent of them had OTT subscriptions versus 62 percent that had cable and satellite.

The draw for broadcast, cable, and satellite is mass appeal. And most of the time, people buy ads based on WHAT (a specific show or channel), instead of WHO (in the case of dealership, you want in-market automotive shoppers). TV ads were (and still are) about mass appeal, getting as many viewers as possible … but how many of those viewers will actually generate a return on your dollar? They're great for "institutional marketing"—getting your brand name out there. But perhaps you should leave that to the OEMs and focus your spend on where the real buyers are.

Let's see how that breaks down for a dealer today. Let's say their CPM (cost per thousand impressions) is $7 for a broadcast ad (a network affiliate or an independent TV station), $20 for a cable channel ad. Well, J. D. Power estimates that only 11 percent of the population is in the market for a car. And that means—poof!—89 percent of the audience isn't going to care what you have to say.

But there's still that 11 percent, right? *Well, remember, these are people who want to buy A car, not necessarily any of YOUR cars.* If you sell Hondas and they want a Toyota, you're once again shut out. And suddenly, that 11 percent has shrunk down even further to a single digit. Plus, you have to reckon with people watching these programs on their DVRs and fast-forwarding right past every commercial, including yours. That further erodes your already-downsized potential audience.

Here's what it comes down to. With broadcast and cable, you end up paying to reach everyone who's tuning in. However, only a fraction of that audience is geared to respond to a car ad. And an even smaller fraction is going to respond to YOUR car ad (if they don't skip past it and miss your entire marketing message altogether). So that means the overwhelming majority of your money is getting flushed down the toilet. So, to continue with the numbers game, your $7 CPM skyrockets to $230 and the $20 goes all the way up to $689, because of how few actual prospects you're reaching.

This is a stark illustration of how traditional media can be grossly overpriced and, at the same time, painfully underdeliver on expectations. So does that mean you leave television out of the mix?

Absolutely not. Let's return to the disruptor in this equation, the OTT services. Some run ads and you can't fast-forward through them. Not only that, but you can also target ads only to those who are currently in-market to buy the segment or brand you're advertising. In other words, no dollars wasted on people who are nonbuyers. Check out the graphic below to see the kind of CPM we can end up with, compared to the more traditional TV services:

A COST PER SALE STRATEGY ACCOUNTS FOR SWINGS IN CONSUMER BEHAVIOR

	BROADCAST TV	CABLE TV	DIGITAL VIDEO + OTT
AUDIENCE TARGETING ▶	BROAD	BROAD	✓ TARGETED
IN-MARKET CPMs ▶	$230	$689	✓ $34

The $34 doesn't fluctuate much (+/- $2/CPM), and you can bank on it, because you know exactly what you're spending to reach actual shoppers looking for exactly what you're selling. You can factor this into your cost per sale in a real and measurable way. It is, by far, the most efficient and reliable spend when it comes to a TV audience.

Knowing three out of four US households can be reached via OTT, and that one in three households have "cut the cord" and are now OTT exclusive—well, going for the OTT option just makes the most sense. *You're fishing where the fish are.*

But let's make something clear: OTT makes a great deal of sense now, but in six months, the most efficient ad spend may be in a completely new medium. Who knows? Just as your inventory changes, so does the media landscape, and again, these are important changes that have to be monitored and acted upon. When a new marketing path opens and offers the best proven ROI, go for it. Right now, those channels are OTT and social media. Tomorrow? Who knows? The only way you will know is to partner with a provider you trust and empower them with the autonomy to act quickly and pivot to what's most impactful.

THE STRATEGY THAT LEADS TO SUCCESS

Remember you're not selling impressions; you're selling cars, parts, and service. Some marketing gurus might tell you their efforts have boosted your impression share up 13 percent, expecting you to jump for joy. But when you look at ALL the numbers, you might see you spent more and sold fewer cars!

It's critically important to look at the right metrics. And that's where the cost per sale strategy helps keep you focused. *The single source of truth is what you're paying per vehicle to make a sale.* With the right data and the right intelligence, you can define what you want your cost per sale to be, set your budget accordingly, and let it go to work, knowing you can pull the plug at any time. When you set out on that path, you'll quickly see there is a direct correlation between increased budget and increased sales. You're putting out more marketing dollars, but the increased revenue and profit more than make up for it.

If spending an extra $500 nets you three additional deals, it's worth it because that cost per sale is only roughly $166. On the other hand, when a high-demand vehicle is basically selling itself, you can pull the marketing plug and either put that money into profits or into offering vehicle discounts that will attract even more customers. Either way, you're saving on your marketing budget. In the first case, it might seem counterintuitive to spend more money than you budgeted—it's probably the exact opposite of the way you were trained to think about marketing. But it works, thanks to what digital can deliver when leveraged correctly. If you haven't flipped the script yet to reflect this kind of thinking, maybe you should. Put results before budget, and let your goals dictate what you spend to achieve them.

Here's a case study that demonstrates how easily your return on ad spend (ROAS) can be measured digitally.

In the old days, of course, dealers were mostly in the dark about what marketing was actually generating revenue. With digital, that's no longer the case. So one of our clients, an automotive group, wanted to develop a solution for its thirty-six stores that would measure their ROAS, as well as provide more of a window into the true impact of its corporate marketing strategy on dealership sales. They wanted to develop a single source for real attribution data and cut the argument on who provided what lead or appointment set rates.

To make that happen, they turned to our PureCars tool, Signal. As noted earlier in this book, Signal is a data-driven, multitouch attribution solution that uses a unique model to weigh the value of digital channels—paid and unpaid—for ROAS and sales. Our client implemented it in all thirty-six dealerships in their network and trained teams on how to use the simple, user-friendly interface.

Signal provided every dealership with instant access to cross-channel reporting, shopper engagement, and inventory performance data to inform stocking, merchandising, and sales. At the same time, the corporate marketing team had the executive roll-up reports they needed to analyze digital channel performance, validate vendor reporting, and benchmark dealers' results.

Armed with that information, this group was able to see a clear link between their digital advertising and vehicle sales at the group and dealership level. They had the actionable insights they needed to make data-driven decisions and efficiently adjust their multichannel marketing strategy to increase ROAS and sales. The result? The group saw greater return on ad spend every month from paid search, display, and social media. Here are a few specific numbers that illustrate that fact:

- +28 percent increased return on ad spend from Google Search
- +34 percent increased return on ad spend from Facebook ads
- +28 percent increased return on ad spend from Display
- +28 percent higher return on overall ad spend

Our feedback from this client was that the information we provided them empowered them to make broad-stroke decisions on which channels and third parties to invest in and which ones to back out of. Their team was better equipped to make more insightful marketing decisions with Signal's data.

As digital continues to develop and evolve, no doubt we'll be able to make even better measurements of ROAS and act on those measurements to deliver even better results.

The next question is how do you determine and target the best and most likely customers for your vehicles? How do you match up your marketing so those customers are the group who sees your messaging? In the next chapter, we're going to help you uncover and connect with your most valuable prospects.

REFLECTION EXERCISES

1. Were you aware of this cost per sale strategy? Do you currently use that strategy in your marketing efforts?

2. Are you still setting your marketing budget in advance? How far in advance? How flexible are you in changing that budget when conditions change?

3. How quickly/easily are you able to change up what you're marketing and how you're marketing it? Are you able to pivot quickly, or does it take too much time? If it's the latter, how can you improve your reaction time?

CHAPTER SIX

BUYING THE AUDIENCE

GOING AFTER YOUR
PERFECT CUSTOMER

Part of Customer Development is understanding
which customers make sense for your business.
—STEVE BLANK, SILICON VALLEY ENTREPRENEUR

An old friend of mine who lives in Detroit wanted to buy a BMW 3 Series, so he asked for my help, knowing I work with a lot of car dealers. I made three calls. First, I got a lease quote from two Detroit area dealerships. Then, just for fun, I tried a dealer in Toledo, Ohio, which isn't all that far from Detroit, and I was a little taken aback by what I heard. The Toledo shop's quote was $30 a month less than the two Detroit dealers.

Well obviously, over the lifetime of a lease, saving that thirty bucks every month adds up to a significant discount, so he made the hour or so drive south and closed the deal in Toledo.

So my question to you is, Who screwed up the most? The Detroit dealers who might have nabbed a new lifetime customer if they had offered a lower lease payment? Well, yes. But to me, the Toledo lot is the real offender. *Why would they offer a more competitive price when this customer is obviously not going to return and service the car with them?* Someone else in Toledo would probably have leased that car from them if they had waited it out. That would have justified the lower payment because the buyer might have come back again and again, both for service and to lease a new car when the contract was up. But as it is, the dealer just gave a substantial discount for not much in return.

This is a reminder of the importance of the cost per sale strategy we discussed in the last chapter. In this case, at least one of the Detroit dealers should have asked where the person lived and offered them a better deal. They could have likely locked in the certainty that the customer would pick their store for service and realized a lot more revenue down the line if they focused on the potential lifetime value of this customer. A first-time BMW buyer is likely to service nearby and continue buying from that dealer. So why be so aggressive on price?

In this chapter, we're going to explode some myths and share some cutting-edge ideas about which customers you want to go after and *how* to go after them in order to keep your sales humming and your bottom line way above water. You won't find much conventional wisdom here ... but you will find new and more profitable ways to consider the complexity of customer acquisition.

FISHING VERSUS CATCHING

Let's start with a simple concept: fishing is hard and catching is easy.

I don't want to start an argument with any anglers out there, but let's face it, fishing can be exhausting. You could sit in a boat for hours and never get a tug on the line. Trust me, that is what it's ALWAYS like when I go out with the kids. Well, a lot of dealers put themselves in that same position. They're sitting in a boat, waiting for customers to nibble on the line, when they should be just catching them left and right.

You might say, well, the objective of fishing *is* to sit and wait. I would argue, *not if you can make the fish come to you.*

How does this relate to auto marketing? Well, some dealers spend a lot of their marketing resources on trying to educate consumers about vehicles so they'll consider buying it. Well, here's a little secret; it's a lot easier to go after buyers *already* looking for the vehicles you have rather than trying to make them pay attention to a vehicle they don't know about or don't care about.

Most potential customers are already educating themselves by checking out cars on the internet. You don't have to do it. They're already taking the time to compare models, options, and prices before they make a move toward interacting with a specific dealer. You don't have to do that work for them, because they're already on it. In most cases, a car or truck is the second biggest purchase most consumers will make over a lifetime, the biggest being, of course, a house. So they want to control the process, and now, thanks to the internet, they can find out almost anything they want before stepping onto your lot.

So why duplicate their work? You're much better off using a low funnel methodology to attract potential buyers who know what they want and are looking for the best deal on a specific vehicle. A low funnel approach means you're narrowing down your pool of prospects to the ones that really count. For example, if you're buying the search term "Used blue Jeep Wrangler Rubicon," that's pretty specific—and pretty much the only people who will be searching on that term are ones who are genuinely interested in getting one. You're automatically catching likely customers by going that narrow.

> A low funnel approach means you're narrowing down your pool of prospects to the ones that really count.

Contrast that with buying the search term "used cars" or even "used SUVs." That's a high funnel approach and one that's almost useless. You'll end up paying for a lot of clicks that just aren't going to be viable leads. In other words, you once again put yourself in the boat with a line out in the water, waiting for a fish to bite. And you could be waiting for a long time.

Smart marketing comes when you think in terms of catching instead of fishing. Attract prospects that are already interested in a vehicle in your inventory, rather than trying to explain to them why they should buy a car they haven't expressed any interest in. Explaining takes time and money, and you can't be sure anyone will listen. Attracting the buyers who know what they want—something specific that's sitting in your showroom or on the lot—is a much more cost-efficient and impactful approach.

WHEN CATCHING ISN'T AN OPTION

Of course, you know full well that there are times when you have a car that's difficult to unload. The kind of car where very few are actively thinking about buying it. So you have the perfect right to ask, "Well, what if no one is searching for what I'm selling? What if no one really cares about some vehicles I've got sitting on my lot?" Well, many dealers' first response would be "Wholesale it fast." But obviously that doesn't really help and is often costly with lower demand units.

We have had to deal with this situation with our clients. We've talked to a few OEMs and niche brands that have been challenged by a lack of search volume. For example, General Motors approached us and asked how we handled their CPOs (certified preowned vehicles). But the problem is the dealers won't make the effort to spend the dollars to certify the cars, because it costs them money while driving up the cost of the vehicles to the point where they're not all that great a deal. Plus the OEM doesn't put any marketing muscle behind them, so the customer demand is virtually nonexistent. For all those reasons, dealers have little incentive to advertise CPOs, and because of all those factors, there is LESS demand in the market for them, simply because a minority of the market is aware they exist. Even if you decided to start pushing them and deployed a search campaign with a half million keywords, that doesn't do much good if there's only, say, six queries or so a month. (Just to set the record straight, some brands are great with CPOs, such as Toyota, BMW, and Mercedes-Benz. They employ a cohesive strategy from the OEM to the dealer that builds demand, justifies the higher price, and delivers the dealer a fully stocked pond to fish in).

When faced with a vehicle nobody knows about and/or cares about, we have to think about stepping back in our Wayback Machines back to 1990 again, where we have to drive awareness. That was most successfully done when you aligned your brand with a consumer's lifestyle, something you see to this day in TV ads from the big car companies, where they portray specific demographics of consumers doing specific activities the viewer would like to do. You, of course, have seen this kind of awareness-building in, say, SUV commercials that show a family four-wheeling in Sedona, Arizona, or camping out under the stars on the beach or a mom able to comfortably carpool a bunch of kids to school. These spots portray positive scenarios where the vehicle in question adds something to everyday lives.

As a dealer back in 1990, you might try to reach your preferred demographics by buying time on a TV show where the viewership matches up with who you want to sell to. As we've talked about, you're missing more than you're hitting with that approach, because who knows how many of those viewers actually want to buy a car?

Luckily, today, we can be much more sophisticated in our targeting.

For example, Porsche, believe it or not, has big challenges when it comes to trying to buy success through search terms. A lot of people love to check out these high-performance cars and see what's new with them but, at the same time, aren't prepared or qualified to buy one. In other words, Porsche attracts a hell of a lot more virtual look-e-loos than buyers.

So … a Porsche dealer might have to go fishing. What do you use for bait? Engaging the *emotions* of those who can afford a Porsche. Who is that audience? That's easy to determine. For example, you can target by income levels and other indicators that someone enjoys luxury products. For example, here in Charleston where we're based, we might want to go after yacht owners, since we're right on the water. Suddenly, I'm reaching a segment that can easily afford our product and generate demand through imagery and videos that speak to the allure of the Porsche lifestyle. I can then execute bidding in my search campaigns that make sure I dominate the competition when anyone from these audiences begin to research a Porsche or any adjacent brands.

Thanks to Big Data, you can reach almost anyone at a micro level. There is plenty of technology available that allows you to target a specific household and simultaneously layer multiple ways to market to it. It's crazy what you can do today, and yet it only hints at what you'll undoubtedly be able to do in the future. So as I said, even though tactically, you might feel like you're back in the 90s trying to drive awareness, you can drill down much more thoroughly on likely prospects using specific outlets to reach specific audiences with certain characteristics, such as income level, past purchasing habits, etc. And through that effort, with some adjustment of the geographic ad strategy, you can generate demand for a vehicle that needs some help and capture it with more tactical paid search campaigns, which can drive huge efficiencies and save tens of thousands or even hundreds of thousands in wasted spend over the course of a year.

Yes, it can get incredibly complicated. But as the saying goes, just because you can doesn't mean you should. There's often an even easier way to find your best and most profitable customers … just by looking within.

DIGGING INTO YOUR DMS

Now, when I say to look within, I'm not suggesting you try transcendental meditation. No, I'm suggesting you go into your DMS and create a data snapshot of your best customers so you can go out and get more of them.

As I said, tactically, you can go after anyone you want these days—by activities they engage in, by their income level, by their gender, by their political views, whether they're married or single, parents or childless, and so forth and so on. There are tons of very cool things you can zero in on to hit whatever ultra-specific demos you dream up. But as the old saying goes …

… just because you *can* doesn't mean you *should.*

Instead, you should focus on the demos that, at the most basic level, represent your absolute best audience. Which brings us to our next question: How do you figure out what that audience is? What do you use as guidelines to find your next "best customer"?

In this case, your north star is your DMS, especially if you've been operating for a long time. Generating reports from that DMS will provide you with defining data in terms of what kind of people continue to do business with you in all departments of your dealership. By analyzing your customer data, you can find commonality in the ones that bring you the most lifetime value, through front-end and back-end gross on car purchases, frequency of servicing, average value per RO, and estimated equity. You can figure out the best zip codes for lifers, as well as the best income levels, age groups, education level, and so forth.

This is where the 80/20 rule comes into focus. The 80/20 rule, if you're not familiar with it, states that 80 percent of your business comes from 20 percent of your customers. By identifying your *current* best customers and nailing down their common characteristics, you've got a baseline to work from in order to add to that lucrative 20 percent. You'll want to send your DMS customer reports to your digital vendor and/or marketing staff to see what data they can extrapolate, how they can convert that data to information (see chapter 3) and act on it. From your DMS info, your vendor should be able to actually create an *avatar* that represents your best customer and tap into a look-alike audience on Facebook or any other major platform that allows this level of targeting. (And clearly, as we've discussed, geography is going to be the most important aspect of that customer profile, as you want prospects that live close enough to come back to you for servicing).

Successfully identifying your best customer avatar should impact not only your marketing strategy but also your actual sales process. Here's how:

Let's go back to the simple example I opened this chapter with. Two dealers in Detroit offer a higher lease price to someone who lives in the area, as opposed to a lower price on the exact same vehicle from a dealer in Toledo. On both sides, the dealers could have done it better. In Detroit, they should have taken into account that this was a local interested in buying and given him a break on the price. In Toledo, they shouldn't have offered a great deal unless they really needed to unload the vehicle, because this person is definitely not going to drive over an hour for service in the future. The moral of this marketing story is to give a potential lifer preferential treatment, because it's worth a little extra expense to get them inside your tent.

Now, let's apply this principle to your own repeat customers. Let's say one comes in and you excuse yourself for a moment to check out what level of business this person has done with you historically. Maybe you find out they've bought three out of the five products you offered them in your Finance and Insurance Department in the past. And they also serviced with you on a regular basis. Maybe that all added up to about three extra grand in business. So ... why *shouldn't* you offer them a better deal if that will do the trick? You can be pretty sure you'll get your money back in thirty minutes after they've been to F&I, and then you'll make even more through the servicing. On the other hand, a repeat customer who bought a car but didn't spend beyond the purchase price will probably continue that pattern. It's not worth as much to cut them a significant break on the sticker price.

In terms of digital marketing, here's what it comes down to. Once you've identified what kind of audience could be of significant lifetime value, you should make a relentless pursuit of that pool of people as well as an integrated approach. By integrated approach, I mean you shouldn't be going after one audience on Facebook and another with your direct mail list. You want who's most likely to buy and service with you, the people who will provide both optimal lifetime value as well as lowest cost per sale and pursue them relentlessly throughout all channels. Most of these channels are in-market audience identifiers. Facebook can do the work for you. Oracle can do the work for you. Google can do the work for you, and so can many other platforms.

> Once you've identified what kind of audience could be of significant lifetime value, you should make a relentless pursuit of that pool of people.

But the foundation of that work is in the fingerprint of your own dealership data. Lean on that DNA, instead of going after golfers, tennis players, or people searching on something as broad as "used cars." Your own internal data can dictate the overall audience, and your vendor can take that ball and run with it. You can also break that data down further and segment the audience by brand (Buick, GMC, Chevy, etc.) or for an individual model, if there are specific units that drive higher margins, F&I revenue, service loyalty, etc.

Now some marketing services like Cars.com and LotLinx claim they have a premium proprietary audience and that's the reason you should spend with them. I think that's an overvalued statement. Their audiences might provide some benefits, but it's not the be-all and end-all. And fundamentally, if you're pursuing an audience and you don't know how that audience fits into your front-end gross, back-end gross, and fixed income gross for that geographic area, or if anyone in that audience represents the "best customer" avatar that is the backbone of your profit picture, then what are you paying a premium for? Not to mention the fact that, if you have defined your ideal customer and are using that definition to drive your targeting, Facebook, Google, Amazon, and Oracle have access to far bigger audiences than the proprietary pipe dreams of companies who have a tiny fraction of their reach.

All audiences are not created equal. And at the end of the day, the most valuable group of prospects is one derived from leveraging your own data that identifies your most valuable 20 percent of customers, breaks down their common characteristics, and gives you the basis for smart, targeted marketing.

OUR DEALER PLAYBOOK

We've been talking broadly in this chapter about how to market to the right audience. Of course, just like every audience is not the same, every dealer is not the same. You have your own specific marketing challenges that need to be addressed, something we help our clients with every day.

Toward that objective, we offer our clients a "Dealer Playbook" that lays out what marketing tactics they should use and when. It's not really a book like the one you're reading; it's a simple breakdown of different marketing goals and how to reach them, on the spectrum from how to drive demand, re-engage it, capture it, and convert it to lifetime value.

To close this chapter, we're going to for the first time publicly reveal the main points of that playbook.

CAPTURING EXISTING DEMAND

Remember, we prefer to catch, instead of fish. It's easier to make a sale when a prospect is already looking for what you have. With that idea in mind, the most cost-efficient digital marketing method is to capture existing demand when possible, rather than trying to create it. That's why we emphasize this should be a dealer's first move.

We capture demand through various methods. Here are a few:

PAID SEARCH

By buying search terms directly related to your dealership or specific vehicles, you're "catching" whoever is looking for you or a car in your inventory. These prospects should be primarily targeted to aggressively win the competitive bidding war in the geographic areas where you're likely to find lifers who will continue to do business with you over the long term. Simple logic.

LOCAL ENGAGE

Optimizing your Google Business Profile or Google My Business (GMB) is a no-brainer, because it's simple and powerful. When a prospect searches for your dealership or dealerships, these listings will populate in a map or on the right-hand column with contact information, hours of operation, offers, and Q&A and can even pull in your entire inventory feed right in the search results page. This is truly the lowest hanging fruit, because these are people who actually want to contact or visit your store. You're just giving them the information they need to do it. Under audit across large dealer groups, we've found that they're responsible for 70 to 85 percent of all phone calls to dealerships. *Google Business Profiles cannot be ignored.*

RETARGETING

When visitors come to your website, they're, again, already interested in buying from you. You've already caught their attention one way or the other. Now, you want to keep it. You do that by following up with a deal, a price drop, or units similar to the vehicle they've looked at on the site. That follow-up could happen through social media, such as Facebook or Instagram, or through a banner ad on another site they might visit, such as ESPN.com, Today.com, etc. In other words, these are people who are already expressing direct interest; you need to ensure you dominate their awareness as they move through their research and keep new inventory and offers front and center. Most importantly, this is the only way you can follow up with 95 percent of shoppers on your site who do not submit a lead or call your store after the first visit to your site. *Ninety-five percent.* Enough said.

CONVERSION

Fail to merchandise, and you'll fail to convert to your full potential. The reality is that the big tech industry (Google, Amazon, Facebook, etc.) are quietly training the consumer every day about what to expect in a trustworthy online shopping experience. If you want a good window into minimally acceptable standards of merchandising, look no further than a product page on Amazon or Walmart. com—good pictures, competitive price disclosed upfront, disclosure of any available sale pricing or incentives, and even payment plan options front and center.

And here's the thing. When Walmart shows a picture of a TV it's selling, it's not sitting in a box out by the loading dock. And yet, many dealerships allow their teams to do just that with their vehicles. Every salesperson who's been trained on walk-arounds has heard the old adage "make the car the star." So why is our online walk around done out back by the fence on some of our inventory? There is a wide array of tools available in the industry designed to help prospects who are undecided to fall in love with your car versus others on their short list. One such tool is one we provide to our dealers called **Value Intelligence**, a bundle of products that can showcase your inventory in a way that helps you maintain gross profits and deliver a world class customer-service experience by enabling your sales and BDC teams with instant access to a wide array of key selling points and comparisons. More specifically, it addresses the fact that the average dealership spends over $2,000 fixing up a used car before they put it out for sale on their lot, but doesn't leverage that expense to their benefit.

Let me explain. Traditionally, the customer is unaware of how the dealer has upgraded a car, In other words, that $2,000 worth of improvements isn't advertised. And I can't help but ask, *why the hell not?* It could mean the difference between a sale and no sale. So we help dealers showcase those improvements through a widget on a dealer's VDPs and SRPs that will detail how a car might have, for example, $800 in new tires, as well as anything else the $2,000 might have gone toward that makes the vehicle more attractive to a consumer. Your merchandising ends up vastly improved, and your sales team is armed with the information that will allow them to make the most of every customer interaction.

Another tool we focused on over the last few years is website personalization. When your website visitor is checking out a specific car or truck, a pop-up offer will show up on the lower corner of a dealer's website that will usually give an incentive to buy the vehicle they are interested in within a limited time frame, in the form of a rebate, cash back, discount, or even a more aggressive offer on their trade-in. The feeling from the customer's viewpoint is they encountered this offer at this particular point by chance, which motivates them to act on it. We typically see dealers' lead counts increase by thirty to fifty a month without spending an additional dime on advertising.

These are the most important actions you can take to "hook" someone who's probably already decided to buy and is preparing to finally visit a dealer to close a sale. By harvesting demand through logical search terms, optimizing your website to achieve the maximum lead conversion, merchandising your inventory in the most powerful way, empowering your sales teams to sell through every dollar of value you've built into a car, and retargeting customers who visit your site with dynamic one-to-one messaging, you're doing everything possible to engage customers actively seeking out your business.

So your next question is probably, What about other prospects who may be vaguely thinking about buying a vehicle but haven't taken action yet? Or cars that aren't in demand? How do you generate that demand and connect with customers who haven't been all that motivated to go to the next step? As noted, that's a much heavier lift, but it can be accomplished through the following three-step process:

STEP #1: AWARENESS

In this step, you're out to answer the consumer question, Which car is best?

Generating demand starts by creating awareness of your store and the vehicles you sell. The best tactic for that is television, either traditional cable/satellite or, as I detailed in the last chapter, using OTT streaming services. As I mentioned back then, OTT offers much more bang for the buck, giving you a bigger, more precisely targeted audience than cable and also allowing instant on-demand reporting on the results your ads are delivering.

STEP #2: INTEREST

In this step, you're out to answer the consumer question, Is the car right for me?

Once you've created awareness, the next step is generating interest from the consumer. To do that, we recommend broad audience targeting through social media, online display ads, and videos. Use branding ads to consumers who have shown interest in the kinds of vehicles you sell but haven't connected directly with your dealership as of yet. These ads can educate the public on why they should buy from you by spotlighting your services, including digital retailing, service pick-up/drop-off of vehicles, enhanced sanitation processes, and other key differentiators in the purchase and ownership experience you deliver.

These "extras" are increasingly important to the car buying public, so don't assume people know about the advantages of doing business with you. Instead, promote those advantages and focus on the time savings, money incentives, and ease of doing business at your store. And, by the way, don't tie the success of this type of marketing to website traffic and clicks. Your conversion rate and cost per sale numbers are much more pertinent to how effective your marketing is.

STEP #3: CONSIDERATION

In this step, you're out to answer the consumer question, Can I afford the car?

The main tactic here is targeting people who are thinking about buying a specific vehicle you have available but may or may not have considered buying at your dealership. Social media and display ads are familiar tactics that should be employed here, along with YouTube preroll and bumper ads.

Finally, we also recommend using the WAZE traffic app that helps users find shortcuts to destinations. Here's how advertising on the app works: when a user's car comes to a stop for five seconds or more and they're within three miles of your dealership, an ad will be pushed to them through the app that promotes some sort of offer, like a discounted oil change at the service department or some other simple thing that might cause the driver to stop by and engage with the people on your lot. You can also pay for search visibility in the app that can drive increased traffic from people with immediate need for service, who are searching for a nearby dealership where they can get it done.

With all these tactics, it's good to observe the concept of dynamic incentive insertion. If that represents jargon overload to you, let me break it down. If someone is shopping for, say, a Ford Focus, then you should be delivering one-to-one creative and messaging with your current offer of, say, a $199 a month lease for a Focus—and doing this consistently across all inventory in search, display, social, and video. In other words, you personalize thousands of different ads with current offers and match them up with the consumer most likely to use it. Tailor a strategy that suits your individual challenges and opportunities.

STEP #4: INTENT

In this step, you're out to answer the consumer question, Am I getting a deal?

You want to assure a prospect they will be treated right at your lot. Once again, paid search is the main tactic here, promoting whatever inventory you need to move through specific search terms related to those vehicles. You also want to again retarget visitors to your website.

There is also a new Google ad asset called Discovery Ads. These are similar in size to Facebook ads, which Discovery Ads were designed to compete with, and they show up on mobile, Gmail ads, and Google homepage ads, as well as YouTube ads. All are valuable online real estate.

Google homepage ads actually do something really cool and powerful. If someone goes to Google.com and if Google picks up that they're in the market, then, before they even search for anything, Google will put a display ad in front of their eyes. So if that person was considering searching on one of your competitors, they just might be motivated to try your dealership instead. All they have to do is click on your ad.

Connecting with the right consumers in the right way is all-important. What's also crucial, however, is to track the results of your marketing efforts using the cost per vehicle sold and serviced metrics, so you can continue to change up and/or fine-tune by tactic, vendor, and creative campaign.

In our next chapter, we're going to take a closer look at how digital marketing gives you a comprehensive and complete picture of how effective your marketing efforts are. Sneak peek: Digital is really the only marketing system that can give you the data you need to make the right calls.

REFLECTION EXERCISES

1. Is your dealership focused on capturing already-existing demand? Or are too many resources being focused on branding alone?

2. Have you pulled reports from your DMS to determine the type of customer your shop should be seeking out? If not, how are you deciding which audience to pursue?

3. Compare your dealership marketing tactics with the ones we've shared in the last section of this chapter. How do they stack up? Should you think about using some of our recommended tactics that you're currently not deploying?

CHAPTER SEVEN

BEYOND CLICKS AND CALLS

OPTIMIZING THE CUSTOMER SALES EXPERIENCE

Establishing trust is better than any sales technique.
—MIKE PUGLIA

A s I write these words, Carvana, the company whose mandate is to have customers bypass the dealership experience entirely, is running a very aggressive TV campaign—*condemning* that dealership experience.

I flinch when those commercials come on, because they feature a car salesman wearing demonic makeup screeching, "DO YA WANNA BUY A CAAAAR?" at terrified customers. As I hope I made clear in the introduction to this book, I love dealerships, and I hate to see this frightening stereotype perpetuated. But unfortunately, it reflects the feeling of many consumers, which Carvana obviously wants to tap into. So instead of looking away from those commercials, we have to confront the negative associations they play off of. And that means taking a closer look at how we sell cars and how we can make it a more positive experience for buyers.

Many are doing just that. There's no question the car business is going through a radical transition period. Yes, dealerships are still brick and mortar, but as I've been stressing throughout this book, more and more of a customer's sales journey is being done online rather than in the showroom. That trend only accelerated during the pandemic, when some customers were actually buying cars without even seeing the vehicle first due to lockdowns.

Transitions require a rethinking and a new vision. When change isn't just imminent but already in motion and you continue to stare into the rearview mirror to see what *used* to work instead of what's going to do the job moving forward, you risk falling behind the competition.

A little while ago, I was on an emergency call from one of our clients. He was upset (as any dealer would be) because their sales had suddenly taken a big plunge. "Something's broken," he said. "I'm frustrated. I'm selling fewer cars than I want to sell."

I responded, "Okay, so did you change anything in the last ninety days?"

"Well," he said, "we cut back on our spending with PureCars by two-thirds, and we removed ourselves from listing sites like Autotrader, Cars.com, and CarGurus."

Something in my head exploded. I thought, *Wait, you did all that, and you're wondering why sales are down? What's next? Turning off the lights, locking the front gate, and wondering why people aren't on your lot looking for their next car?*

In other words, this was a self-inflicted wound. This dealership downsized their own business by cutting their marketing budget and diverting from digital. The results spoke for themselves: suddenly, they were angry there was a big drop-off in leads (more about leads later in this chapter), and we got the blame. That's okay, we're grown-ups and can handle it. But what's distressing is watching dealerships self-destruct like this. We see it happen way too often.

In one case, a dealership began to sell cars like crazy after the younger employees pushed to invest heavily in digital advertising. But the older members of management got overconfident after this new flush of success. They suddenly flexed that "muscle memory" I've talked about before and slanted their marketing budget back toward traditional media again. Result? Same as the story I started this chapter with—a big drop in sales and profits.

I've already laid out the shortcomings of traditional media, but here's maybe the biggest one—what it's designed to do. Traditional media is generally aimed at motivating prospects to come into the showroom, so the salespeople can make the necessary personal connection to engineer a deal. But these days, most consumers make their choice of vehicle and dealership online in advance. As a result, they visit only *one* dealership after they've made that decision, not multiple ones. That change in behavior shouldn't be taken for granted. As a matter of fact, it should motivate you to change some key components of your marketing and sales processes if you haven't already.

How?

I'm about to tell you. In this chapter, I'm going talk about what consumers *really* want from you in the twenty-first century—and most of what they're after needs to be delivered before they even walk through your showroom door. The truth is, there are a lot of opportunities for you to raise your customer satisfaction scores, as well as your sales results, that you may not be aware of.

Read on and I'll identify some big ones.

BRICK AND MORTAR IN A VIRTUAL WORLD

I don't want to sound like a broken record, but dealerships simply can't do business like they did back in 1990 or even 2000.

I've already taken you for a few rides in the Wayback Machine to illustrate the difference between that offline era and today's online one. The problem is, when dealers struggle or face a crisis, they often revert to the old ways even though the effectiveness of them is shrinking with each passing day. The real solution lies with new marketing approaches that reflect today's consumer behavior, rather than yesterday's. I guarantee that there's more than one of your competitors who's doing just that and is prospering from it.

Here's an essential truth that should inform how you view the sales experience in the 2020s: *consumers want it to be as easy as possible.* Just as importantly, they want the merchant to be *transparent and trustworthy.*

These are the secrets behind Amazon's success. That megaretailer thrives because you can pretty much always find exactly what you want on their site and order it with just a search and a click. Not only that, but they provide detailed product information, competing prices from other vendors, reviews, and much, much more. As a matter of fact, they give you so much information, you usually have everything you need to make an informed decision right there on the product page.

Another thing about the Amazon system—to paraphrase *Field of Dreams,* "If you order it, it will come." After you buy an item, you don't get an email from Amazon that it's no longer in stock and the shipment has been canceled. They know exactly how much of everything they have on hand and have perfected a system to get it to you ASAP. So the customer, for the most part, has no worries after they've placed an order. Amazon takes it from there. They even make returns easy. If you're not happy with your purchase and you don't want to repackage and send it back yourself, you can take it to the local UPS store as is. They'll box it and send it back to Amazon without you going through any hassle.

So how can any brick-and-mortar store compete with such a streamlined process?

Well, the Target store chain is doing its best. Now, a customer can place an online order for pick-up at a local store, park at a special spot designated for that pick-up, and have the item brought out to your vehicle. This new service means you no longer have to go through the unpleasantness of wandering through Target to try and find the exact thing you're looking for—and then discovering to your dismay that they're out of it. It also means you no longer have to wait in a long line for in-store checkout if you *do* find what you want. In other words, Target has eliminated a lot of steps in their buying process that just plain waste your time. By doing that, they've successfully leveraged their brick-and-mortar model by creating an online tool that replicates the Amazon experience as closely as possible.

By doing this, Target also promotes transparency and trust. Now, transparency and trust are two attributes that traditionally the average consumer does not associate with dealerships. The stereotype of a shady showroom salesman fudging facts and numbers to make the best deal possible unfortunately persists. As I mentioned at the beginning of this chapter, Carvana, the company whose mandate is to have customers bypass the dealership experience entirely, is running a very aggressive TV campaign *condemning* that dealership experience. But what are they really doing? They are simply aligning their business model with the experience that the retail tech giants are training customers to expect in their everyday purchases and then exploiting a nasty stereotype about dealers to drive their point home.

For example, let's take a look at time. According to Cox Automotive, the average buyer ends up sitting in a showroom for almost *three hours* to purchase a vehicle,[12] even when that buyer has most likely done a lot of online research beforehand. Three hours. It can be hard enough to sit through a movie that long, and that film was made to entertain you. Nobody's really entertaining a customer in a showroom.

And the thing is, there are obvious ways to cut that time commitment down to size. For instance, Cox Automotive discovered that when the dealership enables the buyer to do the paperwork online before coming to the dealership, that three-hour wait shrinks by forty-five minutes. I would submit that over two hours is still too long, but removing that big a chunk of time is a significant drop. Unfortunately, it's still not very commonplace. Which may be why, from 2017 to 2019, the time spent in the showroom declined a staggering ... *three minutes.*

Those numbers may have changed since the pandemic, since a lot of dealership business has been forced to go virtual. But they can easily slide back. Also, as I'm sure you're already aware, for consumers wanting to buy a car, there are more and more alternatives to the traditional dealership process. If you apply a smart marketing perspective to this situation, you can't help but see that if you continue to make customers sit around for three hours, while every other form of shopping becomes faster and more efficient, those alternatives are going to look better and better to the public. The right adjustments can help blunt that competition.

---

12   "52 Surprising Car Dealership Statistics for 2021," JW Surety Bonds, January 29, 2021, https://www.jwsuretybonds.com/blog/car-dealership-statistics.

This comes back to the e-commerce mindset I discussed back in chapter 4. Because so many people now shop online, they've become accustomed to that experience and are disappointed when they can't get it. So when they run into something that smacks of the old pre-internet sales style, they tend to resent it.

THE PROBLEM WITH CLICKS AND CALLS

As I've just outlined, people want transparency and trustworthiness when they go online to shop and compare. What does that entail? Well, they want all relevant information about a product to be posted on the merchant's website—even if that information is negative in some way. They want to know what's in stock, how much everything costs, and what options are available. They can do that with Amazon and a host of other online merchants. But in most cases, they can't do that with a dealership. Why?

Because that dealership is most likely focused on clicks and calls.

Most of our clients let us know loud and clear that they want more leads, the kinds that either prompt a prospect to leave their contact information on the dealer website or call the dealership to talk to a salesperson—clicks and calls. The dealers want people to come to them for certain information rather than seeing that data online. For most consumers, that just adds an extra

> Time is the most precious commodity for today's shopper.

and, to them, unnecessary step. They have to take the time to call, and often, they have to leave a message for a call back. Then they have to go through a whole conversation with a sales rep just to get a couple of questions answered. More time wasted, in their eyes. And time is the most precious commodity for today's shopper.

That's why they want ALL the information at their fingertips. They don't want to go hunting, and they don't want to have to play phone tag with a dealer. I have no doubt dealerships will ultimately evolve to providing all those facts. At some point, they will be forced to, because the merchant experience is transforming right before our eyes and so are consumers' expectations. And as that transformation continues, transparency will have to increase, which mean calls and clicks will decrease. It may come down to this: the consumer will see a button on a dealer website that says the vehicle they want is at the dealership. It may even be tagged as being in a certain numbered parking spot on the lot. When you give the customer everything they need to make a decision, you can win their business without a full court press. That will mean leads will go from a stream to a trickle. Don't be alarmed by that, because that could be a very good thing for you.

I'll explain why in a moment, but first, let me ask a question. What fundamentally would you rather have? More leads calling you? Or more people just coming into the showroom to do the deal? I would think the latter. If I'm looking to buy a new F-150 and the dealership can show me everything about it on the VDP, as well as the pricing compared to other dealers, why would I bother to call or chat with you? Wouldn't I just come to you knowing you have exactly what I want at the price I want on the lot?

You may be concerned about posting anything negative about your inventory. Well, sometimes it actually works to your favor. Bring a Trailer, if you haven't heard of it, is an online marketplace where consumers and dealers can submit their vehicles to be listed for $99, which could be considered an auction fee. If your vehicle is accepted, it will be featured for seven to twenty-one days on BringaTrailer.com. What's different about the site as opposed to a traditional auction or listing site is that they're selective about which vehicles they choose for the site, which means there are a lot of cool and vintage cars to eye. That in itself generates a lot of traffic.

The reason I bring up this site is another big reason they stand apart from the rest: they have no filter on conversations about the cars. So what you end up with is a kind of transparency achieved through crowdsourcing, because commentators are quick to spot any BS on a listing on BringaTrailer.com and quick to let everyone else on the site know about it. For instance, if you list an old Porsche and say it's fully restored and in concours d'elegance condition, within a half hour there will be somebody challenging you. "The M9 bolts aren't coded in the undercarriage!" they might say, or something else that might seem trivial to the average person. For example, here's a real comment on a 1967 Alfa Romeo Spider Duetto listing: "I'll bet a doughnut that it's AR514 (orange red). Remember the car was repainted so it's quite likely got the 'modern' color. It was probably originally AR501 (tomato red on my scale)." So yeah. These commentators have the knowledge base to go real deep into the weeds.

The result of this kind of open forum is sellers know they have to be candid. They know they have to list *everything* about the car— good and bad—or somebody is going to bust them. By sharing the car's defects as well as its positives, a transparent lister instead gets rewarded. They get far more for their vehicle than a traditional retailer or auction would pay out. Veteran eBay listers learned this lesson a long time. On that site, if there is an obvious flaw in what you're selling and you don't disclose it, your seller rating will take big hits along the way, and you'll lose trust. People will stop buying from you. Same thing happens on Bring a Trailer.

Take a look at a listing on that site. Look at all the photos, video walk-arounds, and detailed info that's posted for each vehicle. The merchandising is for the most part outstanding and gives me all the information I need if I want to place a bid. In other words, the site generates sales, not leads. Bring a Trailer moves three hundred cars a week, or over a thousand a month. Wouldn't you love to approach those numbers?

HOW LEADS COST YOU MONEY

Transparency can not only make you money but save you money, as well.

Here's the big drawback with generating leads—it takes time and money to deal with them. Let me skip over to another industry for a moment: airlines. It costs airlines, between human capital and infrastructure, around $35 per call when a customer contacts them over the phone. That's why airlines are pushing chat. A chat interaction with their customer service? That can cost anywhere from one-third to two-thirds less. And most customers like using chat better, so win-win.

Now, let's move back to your business, the dealership. I'd like to talk about one guy who found out for himself how cumbersome leads can be—Rick Ricart, president of the Ricart Automotive Group. A few years ago, he decided to use a trade-in website appraisal tool we were offering, where you could go on a dealer's website and get a valuation on your current car, just by entering a few pieces of information about it. However, before the tool provided that valuation you were after, you had to first give them *your* data as well—your full name and email address (phone number was optional). The objective was, obviously, to generate leads for the dealership.

Well, one day Rick calls and says, "I have six hundred leads from PureCars thanks to your trade-in tool. And, well … I don't want leads. Can you remove that page? I believe the numbers we're putting in front of them for a trade-in are strong, and I don't want to bog down my people by adding another step for them to handle. I want the valuation to appear and then some messaging that tells them if they like the number, come on in."

We did as he asked, and of course, we were curious as to what the effect would be. Once again, a win-win. His car sales did not drop, and his sales reps' efficiency increased, because they were no longer flooded with responding to the leads.

Don't get me wrong, calls and clicks can still be important. But what really matters is answering the questions we've been asking throughout this book: Are you marketing the right car in the right way? Are you marketing it to the right people? Is your market share all it should be for your location? Are you using a strong cost per sale strategy?

> Your marketing should be generating buyers, not leads.

Bottom line? Your marketing should be generating buyers, not leads.

CHAT AND TRUST

I mentioned earlier that airlines and other industries were pushing customers to use chat instead of phone calls to contact them. It's less expensive and less intrusive, and depending on the situation, a rep can actually handle several chat conversations at one time. And as I noted, most consumers prefer chat, especially if they just want to get a simple question answered. For those reasons, chat is arguably more important than clicks or calls. But only if it's used correctly. And our experience is most dealers aren't.

Where are they going wrong? Well, again, they make chat more about leads than meeting a customer's needs. So when a prospect uses chat, the chatbot or the human on the other end of the conversation first asks, "Hey, let me get your name and number in case we're disconnected."

That causes what we in the business call "friction," which results from asking for personal information immediately without first building trust. That quickly puts the customer in a defensive posture, and the subsequent conversation suffers because of it. The customer knows you want their info for sales purposes, and they resent having to provide it just to find out whatever they need to know. On the other hand, when dealers use chat correctly—in other words, they take time to establish trust and don't treat the customer as just a lead—we've found they are extremely successful with it.

I know this sounds completely counterintuitive to how many of you were trained to do sales, but what the big tech companies have uncovered is the psychology of the sales process from the customer perspective. They've learned that psychology through analyzing literally millions of conversations where they're tracking every piece of the data, every word that gets said, and a sentiment analysis of each customer. And the end result of that is smart e-commerce companies have worked hard to deliver a buying experience that's as seamless as possible. The sites recognize you when you come back, and often, they serve you up things you're looking for before you even ask for them, just because they're familiar with your shopping behavior. In other words, the focus is on serving the needs of the customer first, not their own. That's, of course, how Zappos built a shoe-selling empire out of nothing. They made a crazy big investment in customer service and, through that power move, differentiated themselves from all the other online competition in a significant, high-profile way.

So I suggest you look beyond the doors of your dealership and see what's working for other types of merchants. Lose the muscle memory, and take a hard look at how other successful outfits are optimizing their sales processes. For example, real estate. If vehicles represent the second biggest purchase category for the average consumer, buying a home is the biggest. And Zillow has empowered that process for buyers as well. Zillow makes it easy to search available properties and also provides a lot of other relevant information with avenues to research, arrange financing, and complete the purchase process without ever seeing the property, if that's your choice.

All surveys show that what the consumer really wants is a better online experience when buying a car. They want the easy button to take them directly to the information they want. That's why your most important showroom may not be the physical one located on the lot, but the virtual one in cyberspace. The more transparency you demonstrate there, the more trust you build, and the easier you make it for a customer to successfully engage with you, then the more sales you're going to make.

You want to *remove* obstacles, not throw more in the way.

WHEN THE SHOWROOM CLOSES DOWN

When I stated earlier that the cyber showroom is becoming more important than the physical one, I wasn't kidding. Here's an outstanding example of how one dealer group coped when they literally lost the advantage of having an on-location showroom.

We had been working with this particular Southern California automotive group since 2018. Their team has worked closely with PureCars to create data-driven marketing that aligns with their goals to spur growth in revenue and market share. But that effort got stopped in its tracks because of the pandemic. Suddenly, they had to suspend sales operations across all stores due to shelter in place orders.

So the problem became ... well, how do they make money?

The answer was the service department. Their marketing director knew they had to do everything they could to keep customers coming through their service bays while their showroom was closed. But how to get that message out there? Email inboxes were being flooded with marketing messages by other companies in similar predicaments, so that wasn't going to be effective. However, lockdown caused a big spike in social media engagement, so we recommended the auto group spend up on social with a Facebook campaign that had a targeted focus on fixed ops. To pay for it, the dealer group reduced their paid search budget.

The goal of the Facebook effort was to keep their stores' service departments at over 50 percent capacity through late March and April of 2020. To reach that objective, we leveraged CRM data to target past customers due for service or inactive for nine or more months. From there, we used look-alike audiences to expand their reach while still maintaining critical OEM compliance standards.

Working closely together, we successfully executed highly effective ad campaigns that drove a high volume of business in a short period of time at the lowest possible cost. The digital campaigns generated more than two thousand repair orders, making up 59 percent of the group's total ROs during that time. Even better, many of those sales were from past customers re-engaged through social ads. With the average dollar per RO well above $200 for luxury brands, increasing spend in the social campaigns, coupled with historically low CPMs, drove a high ROI and sustained profitability for this auto group. And that goal of reaching 50 percent capacity? Some of their dealerships far exceeded it *with over 70 percent capacity.*

Then there was the store in the northeast that had a similar problem when the state created a host of rules and regulations for how dealerships did business after the pandemic hit. Like our other client, this dealership drilled down on the service department. They reached out to all customers with outstanding recalls, and their sale team suddenly became fixed-op reps and even chauffeurs, driving back and forth to retrieve and deliver customer vehicles for the service department, so that customers didn't have to come anywhere near the dealership to get their vehicles maintained and repaired.

At the same time, they focused on buyers in their immediate area, ones who would bring high lifetime value to the table. Using social media, display, and search engine marketing, we helped the dealership match the right website users to the right buyers. We also pointed the dealership staff to the right metrics to look at when comparing MOM and YOY sales.

Despite pausing campaigns and reducing budgets, conversion rates were up from May through July 2020 from the previous year. As a matter of fact, in May, the dealership exceeded their ALL-TIME sales unit numbers in the history of the store, a trend that continued through June and July.

Both these case studies are similar to that of Chuck Hutton Toyota in chapter 5. The pandemic turned the market upside down, revenue had to be made up outside of new vehicle sales, and fixed ops provided the fix, just as used cars had for Chuck Hutton Toyota. In the case study we just shared, the dealership also targeted fixed ops, but also changed up their customer acquisition digital marketing strategies. In all three cases, in the middle of a crisis, huge opportunities were identified and fulfilled, and financial disaster was averted.

***

In today's retail world, clicks and calls have rapidly been overshadowed by online conversations and engagements—and dealerships should follow suit. Whether that's done through chat, social media, and/or a website that allows for easy engagement and transparency depends on the specific goal you have in mind. The right digital vendor can even help you determine what those goals should be if you're not sure.

So don't get bogged down with following up on leads. Instead, reach out to meet the needs of potential customers, and meet them through your marketing efforts. Remember, it's about catching, not fishing.

And in the next chapter, we'll talk about how to transform your cars into some great "bait."

REFLECTION EXERCISES

1. Is your sales process heavily dependent on leads? Try to determine how much time they take and how many of them actually pan out. Are they worth the time and trouble? The expense?

2. Consider your digital strategy. Does it provide enough transparency? Are you asking for contact information before providing any useful information? If so, think about leaving that element out of the equation to see how your results change.

3. Was your showroom closed down during part of the pandemic? How did you modify your marketing to compensate? Were you satisfied with the results, or would a different strategy have created a better outcome?

CHAPTER EIGHT

VALUE INTELLIGENCE

SELLING YOUR INVENTORY QUICKLY AND PROFITABLY

Price is what you pay. Value is what you get.
—WARREN BUFFETT

I want to start this chapter by talking about eBay, one of the internet's longest-running success stories. Started back in 1995, it survived the dotcom bubble in the late 1990s to become a multibillion-dollar business with operations in about thirty-two countries. Although a lot of professional retailers now use the site, it was built primarily on ordinary people selling ... well, their old crap.

Most ordinary people aren't very sales savvy, which is why eBay has always offered specific advice on how to create the most attractive listings for their clothes that no longer fit, the books they've already read, and some gum Britney Spears may or may not have chewed (yes, somebody actually sold her alleged gum … and then there was the listing for the sandwich that supposedly had the image of the Virgin Mary on the bread). Some of the advice eBay gives users is as follows:[13]

> *A perfect item description is clear enough to tell your buyer what they need to know at a scan, and yet detailed enough so that there can be no confusion around exactly what they're buying.*
>
> *It's vital you're honest and accurate about the condition of what you're selling so your buyer knows exactly what they're getting.*
>
> *Item specifics may include brand, size, type, color, style, or other relevant information about the item you're selling.*
>
> *We strongly recommend providing as many of these specifics as you can to ensure that your item gets maximum visibility on both eBay and external sites such as Google Shopping.*

These all seem like great tips, right? If someone wants to make a buying decision online, they'll want to know all this information before hitting the "Buy It Now" button. And if that info is incomplete, sales will suffer. Worse, if the info is inaccurate, the buyer will end up complaining about the item they've bought, and that will hurt the rating for the individual seller.

Wondering how this relates to selling cars? Well, I'm about to make a bold statement—*often the amount of time and care an eBay seller puts into selling an old shirt for $20 is much more than what a dealer puts into an online listing for a $20,000 used car.*

Throughout this book, I've referenced how important it is to showcase your vehicles in the right way on your website. In this chapter, we're going to take a deeper dive into the science of what we

---

13 "Creating a listing," eBay Customer Service, https://www.ebay.com/help/listings/creating-managing-listings/creating-listing?id=4105.

call "Value Intelligence." This is a subject near and dear to my heart for reasons you're about to discover.

THE EVOLUTION OF VALUE INTELLIGENCE

About a decade ago, dealers really started to advance digital strategy by competitively pricing their vehicles online. Before 2010, it was not uncommon for a consumer to go to a dealer's website or a listing site like Autotrader or Cars.com and see either a price that was obviously too high or no price at all (often the consumer was told to call the dealer to get the price). This was obviously a way to maintain the old dealership way of moving the actual sale negotiation to the showroom floor.

The trouble was dealerships could no longer rely on that old way exclusively to sell cars. Consumer behavior evolved as e-commerce flourished. The likes of Amazon, Zappos, and yes, eBay conditioned us all to expect complete, accurate data on a listing. That was the best way to build the trust necessary to close a sale. And part of that data, one of the biggest influencers, was *price*. Yes, historically, the price of a car was determined by dickering at the dealership. Dealers were trained to try to get the highest price to hold the gross. But times changed, and as we've discussed, over the past decade, consumers began doing more and more of their buying journey online, a trend accelerated by the pandemic.

Now, almost all dealers are using some sort of software tool to guide them in their pricing strategy. That software is designed to tell them how their vehicles are priced compared to similar vehicles in the same market. So let's say you have a used 2018 Chevrolet Corvette. Let's say the average online price for that kind of car is $35,000. Well, if you post a $40,000 price tag for that Corvette on your website, it's probably going to sell as well as a Ford Pinto in the 1970s after everybody found out it had a few too many rear-end collisions that resulted in the car exploding. However, if you went the other way and discounted the Corvette down to $31,000, you'd have the lowest-priced one in the area. It would probably sell that very same day. But your profit would be severely slashed.

Dealers like to move cars. I don't think anyone would argue with that statement. And when they saw how a low price on the internet could speed up sales, they began to embrace that strategy to a point where, if a car wasn't selling after a few days, they'd lower the price to get a buyer in. Now, it's not uncommon today to see a dealer turn over their entire used car inventory in thirty days or less. In other words, in a month or less, that inventory gets fully depleted and replenished.

Only problem? A further erosion of your margins at a time when they've already grown incredibly tight.

However, when constantly lowering prices becomes the primary sales strategy, of course that's going to be the result—and the culprit is the pricing software I referred to earlier. Dealers no longer have the ability to make a lot of gross per vehicle, even when they should. For example, the used Corvette we've been using as an example may be in exceptional condition with tons of options, the right colors, and the right wheels ... and still not recoup its true value, because the dealer was strictly focused on price in order to make a quick sale.

You could also be creating a situation where one hand doesn't know what the other is doing. Your used car manager may have paid more for a vehicle that has a whole lot of bells and whistles, but the consumers checking it out online aren't *seeing* that value. The pricing tool doesn't really take these factors into account, it only "thinks" about year, make, model, trim, and whether or not it's certified. Based on those barebone facts, it gives you the average pricing in the market. Result? A race to the bottom, with cars offering less value competing directly with the same kinds of cars that offer much more value. And that, frankly, makes no sense.

This was a problem I noticed back in 2009, when pricing tools were just gaining traction, and I was determined to address it. I remembered how, before the internet, if you put new tires on a used vehicle, a buyer might come into the dealership, look at the car and say, "The guy down the street wants $300 less for the same car." And all your salesperson had to do at that point was, in true dealership fashion, kick the new tires and say, "Well, that one probably doesn't have new Michelins like this one." The value was *shown* to the consumer in person. Very impactful, but sadly, for the most part ... no longer relevant.

That's because Xers, millennials, and other generations coming up are doing their shopping before they show up at your store. Some boomers have even gotten the hang of this. So you have to *virtually* kick those new tires, so to speak. That's why I developed Value Intelligence, which PureCars offered to dealers to allow them to put on their websites a graphical way of presenting key value attributes. Yes, price is critical, but so is value. So you want to put your best foot forward with great photography of the vehicle and the kind of listing content that will impress consumers shopping for a car.

SHOWCASING WHAT WILL SELL

Let's talk about that listing content. But first, I'd like to offer up Amazon as an example once again to examine how that megamerchant handles them.

So let's say you click on a fifty-five-inch television on Amazon. What's the first thing it tells you about that TV? Well, it isn't that it comes with a remote and has an HTMI cable. Why? Because *every television today comes with those two things.* Instead, the listing emphasizes what you might want to know about what *this* particular television has. And those attributes are generally stacked in a logical way, in terms of the first items listed are ones that make the TV stand out from the competition. For example, is it a Smart TV? Is it 4K? What level of sound quality?

And sometimes, you don't even need to go to the actual product page to find out some of that information. As an exercise, I searched for fifty-five-inch TVs on Amazon. And here is the first listing that came up:

TCL 55" 5-Series 4K UHD Dolby Vision HDR QLED Roku Smart TV

There's a lot to unpack in that heading, but as you probably noticed, it hits the big points right there in your search results, with no extra click needed.

Now, keep that in mind as I return to the topic selling cars. I want you to imagine me coming to your dealership and your salesperson asks me if I'm interested in the car I'm currently eyeballing. And I nod and say, "Yeah, I am." Now, what would you think of your salesperson if they then started off their spiel with, "Well, it has four wheels and tires; oh, and it has glass windows, and, get this, it even has an AM-FM radio!" If you were watching this whole thing unfold, you might pull that salesperson aside and force them to take a drug test to see why their brain just stopped functioning. But here's why I offer that ridiculous example—the features and options on a vehicle are still mostly shown alphabetically on dealer websites. Yes, in 2021, you can start going down the list of what a car has to offer, and the first thing you might see is … AM-FM radio!

Not so ridiculous after all.

Here's what this all comes down to—the same energy dealers have traditionally put into selling on the floor has to be put into selling on the web. Many of you are already doing that and kudos to you. But the second component to this is that it's absolutely critical for dealers to prioritize the relevancy of the content they're displaying. If consumers are checking out your vehicles online, how you present those vehicles will determine whether they are intrigued enough to come down to the showroom, where you have the opportunity to guide them to a sale. Think of the process as all being on one sales track, but remember that the first stop on that track happens 99 percent of the time online.

> It's absolutely critical for dealers to prioritize the relevancy of the content they're displaying.

Our clients have realized this is the case, which is why our Value Intelligence tools are very popular. They take that data dump of features and options that you see on the bottom of a VDP and surface them into bite-size, iconography-based, easy-to-consume imagery that communicates points such as, "Hey, it's a one-owner car; it's priced below the market; it's low miles considering the year of the model; it has new brakes, new tires," all of these little things that can make your vehicle stand taller than other cars on other lots that a prospect might be thinking about.

If we went out of business tomorrow, I know Value Intelligence would be one of the main things our clients would miss the most about us. (Luckily ... we're not going out of business tomorrow or anytime soon.)

THE PROBLEM WITH PRICE DROPS

I want to return now to the topic of doing constant price drops because of those software pricing tools I mentioned earlier.

What we've learned at PureCars is that those tools are prompting dealers to implement those discounts a little too quickly. It's becoming a knee-jerk reaction to a slow day or two of sales. And another thing I see is dealers dropping prices in particular on preowned vehicles at such an exceptional rate that they're not allowing enough time for digital traffic to have the opportunity to view the car at the higher price.

It can be hard to view the reality of that virtual situation without a real-world physical example to compare it to. So let's pretend you and I are partners in a clothing store on a high traffic street, and for whatever reason, we have a shit ton of shoes we need to sell. They've been sitting around our store for a month, and no one is buying. Worse, seasons are about to change, and they'll be out of fashion. So I convince you to do a 10 percent sale to make those shoes walk out of the store. But you're slow to do it. Finally, at 3:00 p.m. on a Sunday, you mark them down. I call you at 5:00 p.m. that same day and ask, "Did the shoes sell yet?" And you go, "No, they're still here." You go home. The store is closed on Monday and Tuesday. I come in Wednesday morning and see all the shoes are still there, and I lose it. "Why are all these shoes still here? Boost the discount to 30 percent off! We need them out of here!"

Should I have taken the discount from 10 percent to 30 percent at that moment? Did I give the shoes enough of a chance to sell before I did that? No, of course not. They were 10 percent off for only a couple of hours when the store was open. There was no way enough shoppers would have seen them and have the opportunity to buy them.

In the brick-and-mortar world of selling, it's a lot easier to determine when to cut prices and when not to. You're in the store, you're seeing what's happening day to day with customers, and after a while, you develop a sense of the timing for when discounts are necessary. But in the virtual world? It's a lot harder to figure out that timing. But the answer isn't automating the process through software. That leads to what I'm talking about: dropping the price before enough potential customers have had the chance to check out the vehicle online. Why do a discount without understanding whether or not that vehicle has had enough digital views? All you're doing is creating more margin erosion for yourself, and it's a self-inflicted wound.

Not only that, but a too-low price can be a danger sign to a consumer. Psychologically for a buyer, there's a sweet spot in the middle of the pricing range within a market that will make a vehicle sell faster. If you get too high above that median, it will slow the sales velocity. BUT it can also slow if you go too far below that midpoint price, because the customer sees that low price and immediately thinks something must be wrong with the car. Is it a salvage title? Has the car been rebuilt after a wreck? In other words, a few price drops can cause a buyer to walk away, rather than get them excited about getting an amazing deal.

Dealers are able to gain the best results in terms of both moving inventory fast and getting the best price possible just by hitting the gas on advertising the vehicles that most need to be pushed, as we discussed earlier in this book. You have to understand what to market and when to aggressively market it. You throttle your digital when a vehicle needs help, and you pull back on vehicles that are in high demand.

Let's go back to the example of the fifty-five-inch television on Amazon. Let's say Amazon has ten thousand of these TVs they need to sell. What are the odds they drop the price before they have the data they need to understand that people aren't going to buy at the current price? The answer is zero. They would never do that, because in their business, the only way they make money is by being smarter than the next guy. Amazon is going to lower a price only if what they're asking right now isn't attracting enough views and sales.

Okay, but what if they have more TVs in stock than they want to have? For instance, maybe they have a ninety-day supply on hand, and they want only a thirty-day supply. Well, if they already have the best possible product page built, then what big lever do they pull to motivate more sales? Maybe getting more eyeballs through more advertising? Let's say they spend more on marketing and finally determine that they have enough consumers looking at the TV … and NOT buying. Because maybe there's a similar TV that's significantly cheaper. Armed with that knowledge, Amazon goes ahead and lowers the price by, let's say, $50. It finally starts selling a little more. Do they cut the price a second time to really get sales going? No. Now they're going to see how well the new price works before cutting it further.

> Determine how many people are viewing a vehicle, and when that number hits a certain threshold and sales are still disappointing, *then* do the discount.

This is the right way to determine price in a digital world. Determine how many people are viewing a vehicle, and when that number hits a certain threshold and sales are still disappointing, *then* do the discount. Think of it this way. If there was no internet, would you be disappointed if a car on your showroom floor didn't sell—if no customers actually came in to look at it? No, that would be silly. You'd instead look for ways to bring more customers in the door, not cut the price on a car nobody even knows is sitting there.

A dealership has a lot of tools in its toolbox to move cars. In a way, dropping prices is the hammer in the toolbox. And if that's the only tool you reach for, then every problem looks like a nail, or, in this metaphor, the price.

What I'd like you to take away from this chapter is the fact that you actually do have a lot of other tools at your disposal, such as spotlighting value, doing more digital marketing, or spending a few hundred bucks on social media instead of dropping the price a few thousand dollars. You can maintain the gross and justify the price, instead of doing what seems easy and discounting the vehicle. You can still maintain the same sales velocity, but with far more profitability.

We proved that fact to our own satisfaction. To evaluate our Value Intelligence service, we did a study a few years ago to see if dealers who do graphically show the key value options, reconditioning, and attributes in their digital efforts have a faster sales process.

It turned out they did. We discovered their vehicles sold days earlier than a similar dealer who didn't display value. Which underlines why I thought Value Intelligence was valuable in the first place: showing a vehicle's value attributes gives the customer *a reason to buy,* beyond price. And again, that increases your profitability as well as making your investment in your used cars pay off.

PRICE VERSUS PAYMENT

There's one more big specific I want to address in terms of merchandising. It's something I feel dealers and the industry in general still doesn't aggressively promote online, even though it's a vitally important one—and that's payment amounts.

As I've been emphasizing, it's important that consumers have all the information they need at their fingertips when they're shopping for a vehicle, so they can understand and easily find what they're looking for. Price is obviously a big part of that information. But something that's more important and more relevant to most? Payment. Because most people shopping for cars are asking themselves, *Can I afford the down payment they want and the monthly payments after that?*

The consumer can't know that simply by viewing the total price tag—whether a car costs $20,000, $22,000, $24,000, whatever the number. Because the average buyer isn't going to show up on the lot with a giant wad of thousand-dollar bills. No, the vast majority is going to buy a vehicle through financing or leasing. So those consumers aren't necessarily as interested in the price as they are in terms of *affordability.* Most already have decided what they can afford to put down and what they can pay every month. So of course, these become critical numbers to consider when they make their buying decision. They've got a budget, and they don't want to bust it.

And yet, those payment numbers aren't the first thing consumers see in dealership merchandising. In many cases, dealers don't provide those numbers online at all, most likely because they see that as part of the on-site negotiation. Unfortunately, that may prevent that on-site negotiation from happening at all. The customer may see the total price and feel a vehicle is not affordable, when it just might be. Or that customer might engage with a different dealership that does provide payment numbers online, so they don't risk embarrassing themselves when it turns out the car is out of their financial reach.

Considering all that, it seems flawed that most dealers don't provide what could be the most critical piece of information for most people in terms of making a buying decision. They have in their minds what they can afford to pay, and just providing a $24,000 price tag gives them no insight into what their payments will be. And because the pandemic motivated more consumers to routinely take their buying journeys online, this omission could end up hurting you a lot. Why would a consumer look at a costly product that provides no insight into if it fits their budget?

So my advice is to flip the script and allow the customer to filter vehicle searches by payment amounts. As I said earlier, you should always think about relevancy with your Value Intelligence. You need to order what you display about a vehicle in terms of most to least valuable attributes. And providing transparency about payment numbers is incredibly important to most prospects.

EMBEDDING VALUE IN YOUR DEALERSHIP

In today's marketplace, the best retailers are the best merchandisers. The ones who showcase the *value* of their wares, matched with competitive pricing, prosper. Those who ignore that value do so at their own peril. Value is a differentiator that can be just as powerful as a price point.

And let me also say that you shouldn't just be merchandising to your customers. You should also merchandise and evangelize to your employees as well, in order to empower them to communicate value. A lot of dealers have a disconnect in their merchandising. They may do it outwardly very well in terms of digitally marketing to the customer, but too often it's not done internally to the same extent. It makes a huge difference if you merchandise to your own teams as much as you merchandise to your own customers.

Years ago, when a dealer had fresh inventory to sell, the used car manager would do a morning lot walk of the vehicles with the sales staff and give them the necessary bullet points. They'd be told things like, "It's $25,000, it's a great color—azure blue—it's got navigation and new tires, and we put in new brakes," so they'd get the ammo they needed to make a sale. Now, with all the listings up on the internet, many don't feel that's necessary—but something's lost without that in-person "introduction" to each vehicle.

Then there's the way dealerships handle inbound calls. Dealers have their phone traffic going to business development centers. These are folks working in the back of the dealership, people who aren't customer-facing, in most cases; they're just there to handle the high volume of phone calls coming into the sales department. So it's seen as a stopgap measure. However, in many cases, this is the first personal contact the prospect has with the dealership, and often customers are disappointed that the employee picking up the call isn't very knowledgeable about the vehicles, especially if they've just seen a vehicle's details for themselves online. If it's a disappointment for them, then it's a missed opportunity for you, because individuals answering your calls are low enough in the sales funnel that they should understand what's attractive about specific cars and be up to date with what's been sold and what's still sitting out on the lot.

Here's how I think about it: at PureCars, if someone presses 1 for sales, I don't want that call to go to someone who's just going to set up an appointment to talk to one of our salespeople. Actually, I really would love it to go to my best salesperson, because someone who calls a sales department has serious intent—it's someone we have a good shot at selling to, if we say the right things.

The great dealers synchronize the talking points they're showing digitally with what their business development center and sales team are using. That can be done in a variety of ways. For example, we offer a showroom app that allows salespeople to see all information visually in a very easy-to-grasp format. How you demonstrate that value is more than just price is by stacking all the vehicle content in the most relevant and accessible way, whether it's online, on the phone or in your showroom. For example, if there's a DVD player for the back that was a $2,295 option when the car was new, why wouldn't you make sure that got some prominent play? Or $200 all-weather mats? If the vehicle has those kinds of extras and the prospect is told about them, they could know they're getting a good deal. Without that info? They might pass on the car.

Our tagline at PureCars for years is this: Value is more than just price. It's a statement we've seen proven time and time again.

REFLECTION EXERCISES

1. How well are you showcase your vehicles' value in your digital marketing? Are you emphasizing the attributes that will draw the most attention?

2. In house, are you communicating vehicle value to your staff, particularly those who interact with customers through chat, phone, or in person? Do they know how to present that value effectively to customers?

3. What is your pricing strategy? Are you too quick to drop prices if a car isn't gaining traction with customers? Do you track how many views a vehicle has gotten online before discounting?

CHAPTER NINE

Q & A WITH DAVID GRUHIN

The View from the Store Level

I t all started with a pinball machine.

David Gruhin is one of today's leading practitioners of digital marketing for dealerships. He's led two auto groups to unprecedented success. And as you're about to find out, his storied career in the car business only happened thanks to that pinball machine.

David is currently the director of marketing for the Taylor Automaking Group, and before I share our conversation, I'd first like to relate a recent success story that illustrates the results that can be achieved when dealers act quickly to target their digital marketing when a repositioning becomes critically important.

We've talked a lot in this book about the COVID pandemic and how it motivated many car dealers to change up their business and create a more robust digital sales journey for their customers. Well, Taylor Automotive was one of those dealers. It was also hit hard at the outset of the pandemic. Sales dropped nearly 80 percent after Pennsylvania issued a stay-at-home order, leaving management with two choices: (1) turn off the lights and go home or (2) roll up their sleeves and start working to find virtual solutions.

Well, spoiler alert, the lights stayed on ... because they launched the following initiatives:

- Video chat

- Virtual appointment scheduling

- Online trade-in appraisals

- New safety procedures to make customers feel secure about buying there, such as free pick-up and delivery.

In other words, they made it easier for customers to interact virtually with them, while reassuring those customers that it was as safe to buy a vehicle during this difficult time. At the same time, Taylor's operations team also trained sales and BDC personnel on the importance of lead response times and revised call scripts and safety-centric contact with prospects.

Then it was our turn. Our PureCars team reviewed real-time sales and service performance, compared this to dealership performance, and measured engaged shopper volume by metro and brand. From this information, we made strategic recommendations to help Taylor Automotive through this crisis. We recommended a budget reduction of 30 percent due to reduced sales and service volume, as well as ways to increase cost efficiencies. We projected they could still effectively tap into available demand even with these cutbacks.

Next, we tailored a strategic reallocation of budget across ad channels, weighted toward a sudden spike in shopper volume on social media like Facebook, and employed tactics that netted the most engagement with the aforementioned online tools.

Result? In April of 2020, Taylor Automotive Group beat the Pennsylvania sales market by twenty-five points, hitting 98 percent of their April 2019 new and used car sales. As for the ad budget cuts, the group increased lead volume by 29 percent, even with a 34 percent reduction in marketing spend.

All this happened for Taylor because David worked with us closely to empower those results. That's why we thought it was important to include this interview with him in this book. He not only gets the importance of digital, but he has the "ground-level" experience of using it in his position at the dealership level.

Prior to his position at Taylor, David was the general manager of Kia of Bedford. As you'll discover during this talk, David had a tough time overcoming dealer blind spots in that role. But now, because of his success with digital, he's sought out for his expertise in optimizing revenue results through innovative marketing tactics.

It's also important to note that David did *not* start out in the auto business. His background was in project management and software management at several large media companies. However, that background proved invaluable when he joined a dealership team, because instead of being married to the ways dealerships had always done things, he offered a fresh perspective that tapped into the new powerful tech solutions available to the average dealer. But it wasn't easy to get dealership staff on board at first.

Read on and find out just how he not only prevailed, but succeeded, despite a lot of opposition. Oh yeah, and there's also that pinball machine …

Tell us how you got into the dealership business.

I collect pinball machines as a hobby and happened to purchase a pinball machine from a guy who was a partial owner of a couple of car dealerships. We hit it off and began talking on and off. A few months down the road, he listed some other parts for sale that I was interested in, so I contacted him. He said, "Yeah, no problem. Come down and get them at my dealership." I'm like, "Okay." I drive out there, and we end up talking in the parking lot for a couple of hours.

At the time, the company that I was working for, Prometheus Global Media, had just been acquired, and everybody was kind of in a panic as to what might happen next. So while I was talking to this guy in the parking lot, I said, "Hey, I doubt you need this for anything, but maybe you know someone who does—so here's a résumé." He starts looking through it. And then he finally says, "Why don't you just come and work for me?" I kind of chuckled. I'm thinking, "What could I possibly do at a car dealership?" I had no concept of how they did things.

But he brought me in a few days later to meet with some of the people at this beautiful Kia dealership in Bedford, Ohio. I walk into their conference room, and there are like twenty-five people in there. It's all the managers from their stores across the group. I had no idea there were other dealerships involved; I had only researched the one before I came in. And I had discovered they had a horrible online reputation. Since I was on the outside looking in, I could only see the surface level of their presence, but the general sentiment about the store was that it was bad. I don't have the exact number, but I'm pretty sure when I had that initial conversation, they had a 1.8-star rating on Google.

I'll never forget the question that one of the dealership owners asked me at that meeting as we were wrapping up: "So if we bring you on, how many cars a month are you going to sell for us?" And I looked at him, and I said, "I don't sell cars. I can bring you engagement and opportunity, what you do with it after that is up to your sales department." I got the job and started working for them as their director of marketing for the stores in the group. And one of the first things that I was tasked with was to analyze their advertising budgets and see what we could do with them.

Well, there was plenty we could do with them. What I came to learn very, very quickly, at least in the many dealerships that I've interacted with, is that everybody knows they need to be spending money in digital, but they have no idea how much or where. And as a result, a lot of vendors take advantage to ultimately squeeze as much money out of a dealer as they can. And dealers have deep pockets. I mean, that's not a secret. And money gets spent willy-nilly on a ton of things.

> Everybody knows they need to be spending money in digital, but they have no idea how much or where.

I was very, very quickly able to reduce the budgets of those stores by $10,000 a rooftop, just at a glance. And it didn't impact *the overall result in any negative way. Then, over that next year while I sat inside that dealership's business development center, I watched how the reps were doing on the phone, how they handled the leads. Because I watched and listened to them, while working with the budgets and the providers who helped generate those leads, I was able to optimize further and really just create a much better situation for the dealership, things that I would have done at every previous job I've ever had. The dealership, however, never had somebody who understood how to do it.*

Trust me, everybody wants to save money, everybody wants to be more efficient. But again, if you're living in an informational black hole, you don't know how to do that. And so I quickly became very, very important to all these people. Unfortunately, a lot of the people at the store were very resistant to me. I was the harbinger of change.

Why do you think they resisted what you had to offer?

Well, guys who have been entrenched in automotive for a long time don't want to hear from the data nerd that they could be doing their job differently, they didn't respond to, "Hey, if we change how we do this, we'll get a slightly better result." It was a hard pill for a lot of people to swallow. Big pushback for a while. But then I remember coming in to a meeting one day where a couple of the owners were there, and ultimately, they said something to the effect of, "Look, we've hit a sales slump. We have no problem with you taking some chances to do whatever you want to do, but it has to be something different than what you've been doing. Go and do that; we'll support it."

So the door was opened for you to change things up?

No, that did not happen. We continued to do the same thing. One day, I came into work, and the guy who I'd been working for as the general manager had been let go along with the general sales manager. I went to ask the guy who hired me, who I bought the pinball machine from, "Hey, what's going on?" He said, "Those guys are out; go downstairs and run the store." And I looked at him and said, "What are you talking about? 'Go downstairs and run this store'? I've never sold car a day in my life. I don't know how to desk a deal."

And his response to me was, "David, it doesn't matter. I have plenty of people who know how to sell cars and desk deals. I need somebody who's looking at it differently and who can help get us to where we need to be. We'll figure out how we're going to pay you and whatever else needs to be negotiated."

I thought, What if I don't even want this? I didn't know. I didn't want to live in this car dealership. And I thought I would be, because the other managers are here all the time. It was weird, so I called my wife and told her what happened; then I asked her what she thought. She was like, "Give it a try; you don't know." So we worked out the particulars, and suddenly I was the general manager of a very high performing Kia dealership in the greater Cleveland area.

What happened from there?

Even with all our struggles and considering we were in Bedford, Ohio, which is not a major metropolitan area but had maybe twelve or thirteen other competitive Kia dealers in that district, we were still top performers, in the top tier of Kia dealers in the United States of America. We were always number one in our district. We were generally number one in the region, even prior to my being put in charge. However, now that I was in charge, I was finally able to do some of the things that I never had any leeway to do.

I immediately leveraged the technologies that were there. Everybody thought that I was crazy with what I wanted to do with paid search. What I said was, "Hey guys, instead of riding this roller coaster of paid search, if we create a budget that we can maintain every month, we'll actually be able to have some metrics where we can track real performance. Month to month, and then ultimately year to year, we'll be able to see what is or isn't working, not just with paid search, but with any sort of digital." That's the great thing about digital. You have all this data that you can use to make smart, actionable decisions, but we hadn't done that. We went outside and said, "Hey, the wind's blowing from the west today and it's seven degrees outside and, oh, look! A sparrow! Let's go and buy this marketing!" That's what we were doing. And the whole thing just kind of evolved into a more data-driven operation. I ran the place like I was running a software development project.

> That's the great thing about digital. You have all this data that you can use to make smart, actionable decisions.

Interesting.

I set up a "bug tracker" tool in the store so that as problems cropped up, instead of whining about them in a meeting, we *could instead log the problem, track it, and fix it. And we fixed a lot of problems as a result of that. I mean, I had buy-in from a seventy-year-old used car manager who was using the tool every single day—which blew my mind.*

I also got rid of time-waster meetings. The three-hour weekly meeting where we played Let's All Complain at Each Other? It went away. Instead, I went to one-on-ones with my managers. We had daily scrum meetings, basically—"What are you working on today? What did you work on yesterday? What are you stuck on? How can we help you?" You know, the things that other, agile type environments do that regularly move the needle and create success. And with that, in conjunction with getting to advertise the way I had wanted to, based on the data that I had been collecting, I got to finally make those last changes to bring on certain vendors and get rid of others.

What was the result?

I don't have all the information in front of me, but when I left, we were the tenth largest Kia dealer in the United States by volume. We doubled the number of cars we were selling, and we didn't spend any more money to do it. And I had virtually the same staff the whole time.

Can you talk more about the obstacles you first faced, trying to get them to embrace digital marketing?

Initially, there was resistance to the things that were just generally entrenched in the dealership. You know, "We use these tools, because we've always used these tools." I wanted to change up how we did live chat on the website. I would be told, "I know the people who own this company; we want to keep using

*them." My argument was I found something less expensive that
had higher rates of engagement. And I think we should give it
a try. Finally, I got them to switch, and we started to see an
engagement list that was quite large. We started seeing more
appointments, and we started selling more cars.*

*Okay, well, I said, "Hey, I want to cancel Autotrader." "What
do you mean you want to cancel Autotrader, we need Autotrader." "Well, if you don't want to cancel it, can you justify
why we spend $10,000 a month on it?" "Because it works."
No evidence, just using a "gut feeling" to run the operation,
as opposed to data and KPIs. We finally did get rid of it. Did
we ultimately bring it back? Sure. But we brought it back in
a way that made sense—spending $2,500 a month instead of
$10,000. And no difference in results.*

*Then I looked at why we were spending thousands of dollars on
Cars.com. Did we understand what we were really getting for
that money? I did an analysis, and it wasn't cost effective. And
everybody keeps pushing back. That seventy-year-old used car
manager says, "No, we need to do it." Well, I can show you that
we don't. Let's try it. And if I'm wrong, we'll go back.*

*That used car manager, at one point early on, made a statement
to me that he'd forget more in a day than I would ever know
in a lifetime about the automotive industry. I finally got him
on my side, even though he'd been doing things one way his
entire life. Ultimately, everybody bought in because everybody
was making more money. Once I showed them that we could
all earn more, then everybody kind of got onboard. And things
ran more smoothly.*

What about traditional media—TV, radio, billboards? How did you handle that aspect?

When I started at the dealership, we had an ad agency. The guy who owned it was friendly with the general manager at the time. They did really high-end work. Our TV commercials looked like they were tier one national spots, but we paid for them, and they were expensive. When I was given the GM role, the first thing one of the owners told me to do was to fire that agency because he was sick of paying for them. I was like, "Okay, great. I can handle the rest of this." And he said, "No, we're going to get you another agency." That agency was driven by the commissions that they were making on media buys. They'd say, "Hey, we should spend $20,000 a month on broadcast TV and $40,000 on radio." And what did we get for it? I don't know! But I worked with that agency, and ultimately, we got to a point where we kind of understood each other. We did spend a lot of money on radio, because our demographic was a radio play all day long, so we were on many stations. It was just a cost of doing business. I want to say that through 2018, we averaged about $120,000 a month in marketing all in, with about a fifty-fifty split between digital and traditional. In addition to radio, we peppered in direct mail, but we did not do much TV. At least not once I was running the dealership.

What did you focus on when you shifted to a heavier use of digital?

When I first started, you know, I evaluated what we had in place, and none of that was actually getting done at all. I ended up meeting Matt Copley from PureCars by accident. I was invited to his presentation by someone who thought I would appreciate it. And you know, I quickly saw that he and I were speaking the same language. I'm like, okay, this guy gets it. What can I do with them? And we went all in on paid search, we went all in on Facebook, whatever they were offering at the time. And obviously, what PureCars offers today versus what they were offering just a few years ago is vastly different, because they keep developing and innovating, which is something that I truly like about them.

But since I met Matt, I think I've utilized PureCars in twelve different rooftops across multiple organizations, and the experience has been solid everywhere. Relative to other providers in the space that I've inherited as other clients that tell me if I spend more, I'll get more, I don't get that from PureCars, much. They understand this is the money that we're working with. So how do we get the most value out of it? And again, using their platform and their people, I trust that I'm getting that answer. And as I said, they continue to innovate and bring new techs, new reporting data, and new tools that really just make my life easier. As a data guy, I spend my time in the week building reports, Google Analytics and Data Studio and cobbling craft together from the CRM, and it's mind numbing.

My relationship with them has now gotten to the point where I'm friends with their director of product. And he knows I was a software guy in the past, so we talk all the time. He asks me, "If you could have a tool, what would you want it to do, Dave?" And we'll go toe to toe on that. "It needs to do this, and here's why, but what if we could give that to you?" They're not only just innovating, but they're taking the feedback, probably not just from me, but I'm sure other dealers as well. And they're trying to bring techs that matter to the marketplace. There's plenty of stuff out there that's being sold that doesn't matter. It's just noise.

I would think anybody in this space would keep innovating. I don't believe you can be stagnant in this realm.

It's interesting that you say that because so many of the other big players in the space had rested on their laurels and were stagnant for so long that other entities came in and did some market disruption, which is why you see what's happening now in automotive—especially because of the pandemic. I mean, look at what happened with digital retailing and cars, because dealerships finally had to get on board. If not for the pandemic, high-level digital retailing would be probably another five to ten years off, unless Carvana and Vroom really figured out how to stick it to dealers.

Well, Carvana's TV campaign featuring demonic car dealers is really something.

The general sentiment about car dealers is somewhere in that realm. For as many people who had a quality experience at a car dealer, there are probably five who didn't.

Is that something you tried to address in your years at dealerships?

Absolutely. Absolutely. Like I said, we were a 1.8-star rating dealership at Kia Bedford when I started there. By the time I left, we were four-point something, I want to say a 4.5. I shot for 4.8, but we had some issues where a lot of our buyers were subprime. And as a result, being subprime and needing to fix their cars, we got a lot of hate in the service department when it was time to pay the bill.

But we swung the needle in the totally opposite direction with our customer service. I actually empowered the people in the store who used to come running to me with, "Hey, I got a customer who's got a problem. Can you help me fix this?" What I finally told them was, "Listen, if you can fix that customer's problem for a hundred bucks or less, go ahead and do it. You don't have to ask." Because at the end of the day, saving the hundred on the front side cost us five times as much in aggregation, letting the problem just float out there in the ether.

We implemented other dealership tools to really motivate our client base to give positive reviews. Now, sometimes that doesn't work out, because those tools could ask everybody for reviews with no discretion whatsoever. But then again, getting a bad review sometimes is a good thing, because it helps you uncover potentially a systemic problem at your store that you can root out. I started seeing a lot of trends in certain reviews that all pointed to either the same department or sometimes the same individual. So you can use those reviews as a coaching moment to fix a problem. You can ultimately use those reviews as a way to weed out the people who don't want to get on board. Yeah, the marketing is important—how you contact somebody, how you get them to the store, how you sell him the car, all of that. But how you treat them is so much more important, especially when everybody else is marketing to your person to try and get them to jump ship and come buy from them instead of you.

Not that we didn't. We used the platform AutoAlert to make sure that we were working to find cars that people were driving. We could get them out of the interest rate they were in, we could maybe lower their payments, whatever it was that would help customers do what's good for them, but what was also still in the best interest of the store, which is to maintain that relationship.

After you left Kia of Bedford, you went to Matt Taylor Auto Group. How was your experience there?

Diametrically different. The owner of the group, Matt Taylor, and I work closely together. He is involved in the day to day at all of his rooftops. He is interested in what the data is telling him. He wants to make smart decisions, utilizing that data. And we have done that. We have used the data at hand and also employed newer technologies that are now available to us to dive even deeper, to make the best possible decisions. And we just had one of the strongest years the group has ever had. We fully embraced the digital retailing. There was no resistance. When the COVID pandemic hit, we went headfirst into strong digital messaging to make sure that everybody understood what we were trying to do to keep people safe.

So what is the marketing mix at the Matt Taylor Group now? Is it still fifty-fifty with traditional and digital?

It depends on the store. We're actually a little bit heavier on digital overall, and I think that has a lot to do with the demographics in the area. However, we were still doing newspapers at one of the stores, because the demographic is right, and it worked. When somebody brought it up, I said, "I'll try it. We'll just keep track of what's going on." And we just make sure that we're tracking people who bring in those newspaper offers. We are definitely slanted more toward digital, but the mix changes from month to month.

We make a lot of moves in the Taylor Group, and sometimes we make them a little too fast. In my opinion, I want to have a little bit more data to make sure that we're making the right move or at least as close to the right move as possible. But sometimes we get excited by that shiny new thing that's out there, and we want to give it a try and do that, but we try not to increase our budgets. So we have to shift money from somewhere.

Looking toward the future, is there still a place for traditional media?

Absolutely. The general manager I worked with when I first got into auto told me, "Dave, if you want to ditch all the traditional marketing, let's just go ahead and do it. Whatever you want to do." And my reaction was, "Look, I come from media groups; these things are not mutually exclusive." They help reinforce each other. Right? I know people live on their cell phones now more than ever, but they do still watch TV, and they still do listen to the radio when they're driving. And if you can reach those people that way, you have more opportunity to ultimately engage with them at some level, and hopefully we can convert them from there. Now, what I will say is that traditional is probably going to look a little different in the coming years as more and more people adopt connected TV and OTT services. I look at that as, yeah, you can track those things a little bit more, but at least right now, most of my dealers that I interact with still perceive that as a traditional play. It's a video on a screen, like TV. So it's a traditional thing.

What do you see on the horizon in terms of digital marketing for dealerships? Any exciting new developments you're anxious to take advantage of?

Well, right now, we've hit this precipice, right? People want to interact with car dealers in a totally different way. And we're still adapting to that. Digital retailing is just one portion of it. How else can we interact with the customer on their own terms? And if the technology is driven toward satisfying that for the customer, ultimately, we're going to see continued engagement. We're not going to lose the business to the Carvanas that tell consumers, "Hey, we're totally hands-off. We'll deliver a vehicle. Or you can pick it up." Great. That's fantastic. Until your car breaks down, right? Where do you go to get it fixed? Who do you trust? At the end of the day, dealers can replicate the Carvana experience, as well as provide service when you need it. We're also accountable. But dealers who haven't embraced not just digital retailing but also a digital customer service model are going to be the dealers that ultimately get left behind, because that's what everybody is looking for. Again, that reaches across multiple verticals. Customers want to know, How do I get exactly what I want in the friendliest way possible? Where, if I have a problem, can I get the best help I can get with the least amount of resistance? Dealerships have to position themselves to deliver that kind of positive experience.

CONCLUSION

What's dangerous is not to evolve.

—JEFF BEZOS

Traditionally, selling vehicles has always been its own thing. The dealership sales process has always been largely siloed from "normal" merchant practices. When consumers went to stores and malls, they would never stand for sitting around and haggling over prices and financing for hours. But that's exactly what they conditioned themselves to expect when they planned to go buy a car at a dealership, because that's just how it was done—even if they knew ahead of time what kind of wheels they had in mind. While losing a whole afternoon that way wasn't anybody's idea of a good time (except maybe mine), it all came down to this:

What choice do we have?

> The dealership sales process has always been largely siloed from "normal" merchant practices.

Since pretty much any dealership they went to would treat them the same way, consumers submitted to the process. But over the last twenty years, the way things had always been done has slowly been going the way of the dinosaur. First of all, buyers could find out almost anything about a vehicle, including what the price *should* be, just by doing a few searches on their smartphones. They didn't have to come to a dealership for information, only to do the final transaction. But in spite of that, most still found themselves sitting around waiting for hours just to accomplish what should have been simple and relatively easy. They were the victims of dealers' muscle memory, which caused them to stick to the burdensome way things had always been done, instead of looking to other innovators in online marketing for new and improved ways to attract new customers and retain existing ones. It's understandable, because, let's face it, change takes effort and old habits die hard.

Then came the pandemic.

In many states, showrooms were completely closed down for periods of time, so there was no choice but to embrace radical change through digital tactics. And as you've seen in several case studies we've included in this book, many dealerships made a stunning discovery when dealing with the COVID crisis: doing things differently could not only work but could also help a store prosper like never before, if they just focused on the right things. For example, if you found yourself suddenly without new cars to sell, the answer was to focus on your used car business. If people were nervous about coming into the showroom, the answer was to focus on fixed ops. In other words, when one revenue stream was threatened, then another one needed to be bulked up to compensate. And the only way to pull off this kind of major retargeting quickly and effectively was through digital.

It also brought a much-needed reminder to dealers to attend to the care and feeding of a very important figure they too often tended to overlook over the years—the customer.

In a way, dealers have taken the customer for granted for too long. For generations, America has been about *driving*. While mass transit worked in places like New York and Chicago, in the vast majority of the country, people have always had to buy cars in order to get from one place to another. At the same time, dealers worked out sales processes that worked best for themselves, not the customer, who ended up with no way to enter a dealership without being at a disadvantage. That left the dealerships with the overwhelming edge in the negotiation, but that edge is rapidly diminishing, along with margins.

That's because consumers have been trained to expect more today from those they buy from. They expect companies to cater to them, to provide transparent and relevant information about the products and services they're considering, and to make the actual transaction as painless as possible. And this is where it's all too easy for dealerships to drop the ball.

> **Consumers have been trained to expect more today from those they buy from.**

We can no longer silo our method of selling vehicles from how other companies sell clothes, books, furniture, etc. We must grow and adapt beyond the muscle memory of what was done in the past. We must shine a light on the blind spots, so we can fully see how twenty-first-century car marketing *should* be done. And to do that, we have to develop what Jeff Bezos calls "True Customer Obsession." He explains it this way:

> *"There are many ways to center a business. You can be competitor focused, you can be product focused, you can be technology focused, you can be business model focused, and there are more.*

But in my view, obsessive customer focus is by far the most important. Even when they don't yet know it, customers want something better, and your desire to delight customers will drive you to invent on their behalf."[14]

This is the philosophy that enabled Bezos to build a $1.7 trillion empire and the largest disruptor in the e-commerce space. Hell, even in the *regular* commerce space. I've referred frequently to the Amazon model throughout this book. That's because it's a model I admire and it's a model I've seen work time and time again for our clients. His customer acquisition strategy, how he works his ad budgets and how he tailors the shopping experience to what the customer wants rather than what Amazon wants are all huge game changers for any business that adopts his mindset.

So I am hoping everyone reading this book who's associated with a dealership won't just go on with their lives after they finish it. In fact, I'd like to challenge you to take action. If you found the ideas within these pages compelling and worth a try, share the book with your associates. If the blind spots we describe resonate, set out to address them with your coworkers. And if you've only reluctantly embraced digital marketing up until this point, go all in on it. Don't think about it as something that's coming in the future—because it's right here, *right now*. And if you don't have a digital expert in house or a vendor who can deliver the right results for your store, you're at risk of losing ground, if you haven't already. (And BTW, when you do decide to get some added expertise on board, be careful. There are a lot of people out there who will drop a lot of data in your lap that you literally won't know what to do with. You need professionals who

---

14   Sonia Thompson, "Jeff Bezos Just Explained How to Achieve Customer Loyalty in Only One Sentence," Inc. magazine, August 29, 2017, https://www.inc.com/sonia-thompson/in-1-sentence-jeff-bezos-explains-the-philosophy-e.html.

can give you actionable information, grounded in facts, that will give you clear-cut digital strategies, not a PDF filled with numbers that just make your eyes spin around.)

The more you focus on a positive customer experience in all areas of your dealership, the more new customers you'll win and the more loyalty you'll inspire in your existing ones. They in turn will be evangelists for your business, preaching your good works and bringing in even more buyers.

Blind spots can be overcome. We know that from experience. The only question is, are you willing to look at your own? Take a hard look and work to overcome them. If you do, I guarantee you'll be blown away by the results.

Printed in the USA
CPSIA information can be obtained
at www.ICGtesting.com
JSHW012032140824
68134JS00033B/3005